religion

and personality

alba house
a division of St. Paul Publications
STATEN ISLAND 14, NEW YORK

problems

mental
health
series
2

BY REV. E. F. O'DOHERTY, M.A., B.D., PH.D.

Nihil Obstat:
Edward J. Montano, S.T.D.
Censor Librorum

Imprimatur:
Francis Cardinal Spellman
Archbishop of New York

February 20, 1964

The Nihil Obstat and Imprimatur are official declarations that a book or pamphlet is free of doctrinal or moral error. No implication is contained therein that those who have granted the nihil obstat and imprimatur agree with the contents, opinions or statements expressed.

Library of Congress Catalog Number 64-15373

Designed, printed and bound in the U.S.A. by the Pauline Fathers and Brothers, Society of St. Paul, Staten Island, N. Y.

contents

ACKNOWLEDGMENTS

The essays in this book, somewhat altered in some cases, appeared in the following journals:

Studies, Dublin (chapters I, III, IV, VI, VII, IX, X, XI, XII, XIII)

Irish Theological Quarterly (chapter II)

The Institute of Chemistry of Ireland Journal (chapter V)

Doctrine and Life (chapter VIII)

To the editors and publishers of these journals, I should like to express my gratitude for their ready permission to republish.

E. F. O'D.

1 religion and mental health

The idea of mental health means a great deal more than the
mere absence of mental illness. It connotes a degree of maturity of mind and emotional development commensurate
with an individual's chronological age. It demands a high
level of integration of the personality; it means judgment
freed from the distortions due to emotional pressure, and
consciousness freed from an obsession with self. It demands
a degree of extroversion which yet leaves sufficient room for
introversion in the form of insight leading to self-knowledge.
And finally, for our purposes here, it demands good interpersonal relations: with oneself, with others and with God.

Traditionally, theologians have spoken of "natural religion", in the sense that somehow an acknowledgment of, reverence for, and sacrifice to God is natural to man, together
with collective ritual or symbolic behavior springing from the
same source. Revealed religion—the true faith—does not take
away nature, but perfects it. So that if there is any truth in
our contemporary picture of the mind and its functions, conscious and unconscious, this must have been known to God
and His Revelation must have been made in accordance with
it and with our capacity to receive. There can be nothing in
His Revelation, and therefore nothing in His Church, its

teaching, and its practice, which of itself could conflict with the exigencies of our nature or interfere with mental health in the sense defined.

Why is it therefore that one meets so many problems in practice in which religion and mental health seem to be in conflict? It is not enough to say that the fault lies within ourselves. This is true in as much as there is some predisposing factor in the individual which produces a mental health problem. But why should religion, or religious teaching or practice, precipitate a problem?

Religion should serve as a great integrating force in molding the personality and producing fully healthy mature beings. Why is it therefore that we seem often to produce negativeness in the children to whom we teach religion? Why is it that just at the point where religion should begin to be really meaningful—the late teens, when intellect has reached its peak development—at this very point, it seems so often to lose all meaning, or at any rate to lose all efficacy in affecting behavior? Why is it that religion, which in the words of Our Divine Lord, says to us "Fear not, little flock", seems instead often to generate anxiety:—not the "fear and trembling" in which we are to work out our salvation—but the anxiety of neurotic guilt? Why is it that scruples, a spiritual trial, are so closely linked with the natural illness called compulsive-obsessional neurosis that even a good and experienced confessor fails at times to distinguish the two? Why are holy people often very difficult human beings, if religion should be an integrating and maturing force? Why is there so often a religious content in the manifestations of the mentally ill?

I suggest that among the many factors which are relevant to a solution of these problems, there are two which concern us deeply. One is the emotional charge with which we sometimes load our religious teaching, and the other is the fact that we tend to import into our religious belief and practice elements which on examination we must admit have no place there.

In general, mental illness is a pathological condition of the emotions, or of the imagination, or of both emotions and imagination. It is not an illness of the soul or of the intellect, but it can fetter the soul and cripple the intellect: that is to say, a mentally ill person is working against a great handicap in the spiritual life inasmuch as he is limited in freedom to the extent to which he is ill. A neurotic condition admits of all degrees of severity from the almost indiscernible mild sort of thing which most people experience at some time or other, to the very marked condition of the major hysteric or hypochondriac. But, mild or severe, it always involves conflict— with oneself, with one's neighbor and with God. These are so inter-related, both in reality and in thought, that you cannot disturb one element without disturbing the pattern as a whole. A disturbance of this pattern produces any one or any combination of the following: anxiety, egoism, infantile dependence, immoderate aggressiveness, depression or feelings of "despair", a sense of being "shut-in"; distrust of others, or a sense of being persecuted, or at any rate unjustly treated, and certainly misunderstood; self-depreciation (mistaken for humility), tears of self-pity (sometimes mistaken for the "gift of tears" that spiritual writers speak about); and finally for our purposes here, emotional rigidity or apathy, often mistaken for strong-mindedness and self-control.

It is important to remember that neurotic conflict is (at least to some extent) unconscious, and its effect on consciousness, and therefore on behavior, is involuntary. The result is that exhortation from without to more intense moral endeavor is very often, if not always, fruitless. The pressure of the conflict on consciousness must be eased first, either by resolving the conflict entirely, or at least by making its source fully conscious so that its relevance and influence can be understood; or, in an older terminology, so that the individual's behavior (including his thought-processes which are for the moment governed by irrational forces) may be brought back under the control of reason. There is a sense in which this is much more a matter of fundamental education of the personality than of therapy applied to an illness.

According to one school of analysis, religion itself is regarded as a neurosis. According to another, neurosis is precipitated by the absence of religion. According to the former view-point, religion is generated by our inability to allay our childish and infantile fears. It is essentially, in this point of view, a refusal to cope rationally with reality, an escape, a refuge. It involves the repression of our fears and the projection of our fantasies. It thrives on rationalization, and all its solutions to life's problems are rationalizations. According to the other school of thought, religion represents the seizing of our consciousness by essentially irrational forces of the unconscious, which somehow makes life livable and valuable, and produces mental health. Both these points of view are false, and it is hardly necessary to explain how and why they are false.

But where you find error, it is rarely without some admixture of truth. Freud's line of reasoning was that since he could discern in the genesis and practice of religion the processes of repression, projection, rationalization and the rest, that therefore religion was explained away and shown to be an illusion. It is equally arguable, however, that if the processes of repression, projection, rationalization and the rest are as widespread, or as connatural, as Freud claimed they were, then one should not be surprised to discover their traces, even their necessity, in true religion, and to find manifestations of them in those who believe and practice the true religion. Our nature is not changed by the act of faith: *gratia naturam non tollit.*

There is no doubt, for instance, that religion of any kind, and therefore *a fortiori* true religion, can be a very potent defense against anxieties, unconscious and childish fears, and especially the fear of death. But the truth or otherwise of religion must be established independently of its functioning as a defense against fears. The fact that we need defenses against fears might bear out Jung's contention that we need some form of religion for mental health. But it certainly does not establish Freud's contention that religion is therefore a neurotic manifestation.

The fact is that our religion, like any other, can be used to allay our natural fears and anxieties, but this is not its formal function precisely as a supernaturally revealed true religion. Neither is it the essential function of revealed religion to comfort us, and ease our pain and sorrow. We recognize this in regard to bodily ills and material misfortune, so that we do not apply the false criterion of material progress as a way of deciding the merits of different religions. But we may be inclined to forget that freedom from anxiety and the comforting of sorrow are material benefits, too. There is no doubt that religion can and does console and comfort and strengthen. But these are not its essential function. If we sometimes attach too much importance to these are we not perhaps indulging in a little infantilism?

I suggest that sometimes we may be inclined to stress these "natural" benefits of religion unduly in the minds of those we teach. For some this will be helpful, even indispensable. For others, however, it may be disastrous. Many times one has heard from young adults phrases such as:

"I am not afraid to die, so why should I need a religion?", or "Religion only increased my anxieties instead of allaying them". It might be very important to stress the fact that religion taken seriously will undoubtedly increase one's anxieties.

But it is the other aspect of Freud's thesis that I should like especially to stress: the fact that sometimes we may be tempted to use our religion, or to let others use it, as an escape, or as a means of projection or rationalization. There is no reason to expect among people striving to lead good lives, nor even among religious, a higher percentage of normally balanced minds than one finds throughout the rest of the population. If anything, there are reasons for expecting a higher percentage of maladjusted people, at any rate under certain conditions, and of immature personalities, or dependent personalities, who lean for support on religion. This means that one should be neither surprised nor scandalized to find good serious-minded devout individuals manifesting strange symptoms at times. There seems to be little doubt that people sometimes use religion as a way of refusing to cope rationally with reality. The most obvious example of this sort of thing is perhaps the Christian Scientist refusing medical aid when he is ill. But it is at least possible that we ourselves may on occasion be guilty, in the name of faith, of escaping from reality in analogous ways. It is difficult at times, observing people's behavior, to draw the line between escapism and rationalization on the one hand, and genuinely deep faith on the other. Probably the more usual thing is a mixture of all these factors since, as Professor Nuttin of Louvain says, "Human motivation is never purely rational or purely spiritual".

Let me indicate some of the ways in which rationalization may appear. If we are in difficulties, we should have recourse to prayer. This is a clear obligation of the Christian way of life. But if we leave the difficulty because it is difficult, and start to pray because it is easier than coping with the problem, we may be rationalizing in a big way. Obviously one should have recourse to prayer while trying to cope physically with the problem. Sometimes at least, our prayer savors of wishful thinking, and sometimes, I fear, we communicate this rather unhealthy attitude to our children. Again, in the matter of difficulties and temptations, it is important to remember that it is not only the devil who tempts us, but the world and the flesh are also active—by which is meant ourselves and our environment. I do not suggest, as non-Christians have frequently suggested, that we use the devil as a bogey-man with which to frighten children. He is very real and certainly to be feared. But I do suggest that sometimes we rationalize our own difficulties and responsibility by blaming on him matters which spring from within ourselves. The fault, sometimes at least, lies within ourselves, neither in our stars nor with the devil.

We rationalize also in other ways. It is inevitable that when the human mind reaches a certain level of maturity it will begin to seek explanations of problems and even of the mysteries of religion. Obviously one should not confuse a difficulty with a doubt, and few in fact make this mistake. But together with the *Credo ut intelligam* of St. Anselm one should remember the *Intelligo ut credam* of St. Augustine. It is better to seek an explanation of a difficulty than to refuse to acknowledge that it is there. In the spiritual life there is a point at which faith is purified by the withdrawal of consolation and all temporal aids of faith, so that the will clings blindly to the fact of God revealing, and the understanding seems to be clouded. Not all souls reach this stage, however, and it is rationalizing in a big way to account for the minor difficulties the intellect encounters by supposing one is going through a purification of this kind.

There are other ways in which we import into our religion, or at any rate into our attitude towards it, elements which properly belong in the context of unhealthy thinking. The compulsive-obsessional states for example are characterized by repetitive, ritualistic patterns of behavior, easily identifiable when the condition is very marked. When the condition is less marked we do not notice the compulsive element and very often it is difficult to distinguish between this compulsive factor and the simple formation of habits. The difference can be put fairly simply like this: a habit is a facilitating mechanism which for good or ill makes the carrying out of an action easier and sometimes automatic. But in the compulsive condition emotion predominates, usually the emotion of fear, and it is this which determines the subsequent behavior. Thus an action which proceeds from irrational fear of the consequences of its omission partakes of an unhealthy compulsive character. May one suggest that sometimes at least some good people exhibit a compulsive-obsessional quality in their religious practices? Instead of praying, for example, to glorify God, or even to supplicate His mercy, it is easy to fall into the frame of mind where one says a great many prayers because to omit a particular prayer we have adopted would be visited by dire consequences. It is impossible in a brief treatment like this to draw all the proper distinctions accurately, and I do not wish to suggest for a moment that all good people are guilty of formal superstition, but I think it is important that we should not exhibit in our practice of religion any element which even remotely savors of the superstitious. Apart from the theological aspect, it is bad from the mental health point of view.

Very few of the "difficulties about religion" which manifest themselves in late adolescence or early adulthood are really "religious" or "theological" difficulties. Most of them are either moral problems or mental health problems, or a combination of moral and mental health. In other words, what appears to be a religious problem is a manifestation in a religious context of some aspect of mental life with much wider and perhaps deeper ramifications.

The sixth commandment is an obvious context in which an apparent religious problem will appear. The difficulty primarily is a moral one, perhaps, which precipitates an emotional one—fear, or neurotic sense of guilt, or a compulsive-obsessional attitude, or desire (desire is also an emotion). Sometimes the young person in this condition has recourse to rationalization. His thinking might be expressed by "I cannot help it anyway", or "It cannot be wrong because it is so natural", but more often he has recourse to projection: the attributing to some other thing or person of the responsibility for one's own condition. Thus he may say: "I would not have this fear, or this sense of guilt were it not for God, or the Church, or the priests, etc." The next stage is easy. First fearfully, and then more consciously he begins to deny the existence of God, or to repudiate the Church. Since the rejection of God or of the Church takes place on an emotional basis, and not on an intellectual one, rational arguments for the existence of God, or lectures on the historicity of the Gospels and the notes of the True Church will often have little or no effect.

Sometimes again the process is even more "psychologically" colored than this. A child's attitude to his father, for instance, is very relevant in understanding his later attitude to God. Freud drew attention to this fact and showed how the "introjection of the Father-figure" affected one's mental and emotional attitude to God. He thought that he had thereby "explained away" the existence of God. This of course is a non-sequitur in elementary logic. The problem of the existence of God is obviously independent both of the genesis of the idea of God in the child's mind and of his emotional attitude towards Him. But the child's emotional attitude to God is certainly affected by his attitude to his father and to authority generally, and therefore helps us to understand something at least of the religious revolt or adolescent atheism of young people. For if in the natural order we have come to dread the notion of father, to fear him, to regard him only as the source of frustration and repression, it is only psychologically natural to suppose that we may import something at least of these attitudes into our attitude to God.

Grace does not destroy nature, and the spirit whereby we cry Abba, Father, will be colored by the affective tones which the word bears in the natural order. Thus, it would appear that some at least of those who go through a period of religious revolt in the late teens are not experiencing a formally religious problem but are going through a struggle on the natural plane, perhaps in the deep unconscious, for emancipation from an emotional conflict. This is not to relieve them of all responsibility for their present attitude. Their acceptance of atheism or irreligion may still be very culpable indeed. Giving a natural cause for their attitude does not mean that their acts are wholly "determined" by such a natural cause. If it is known for instance that a young man has become a profligate because of his association with bad companions, this does not mean that we thereby relieve him of responsibility for his profligacy. But it does give us a lead as to how we might set about straightening things out. First, obviously and if possible, get rid of the distorting influences. In the same way in the sort of case under consideration, instead of considering the atheism or irreligion as the immediate point to be tackled, the first thing to be done is to relieve the emotional pressure. Then it may be possible to deal with the theological side of things.

The father is not the only source of emotional conflict and resentment, however. The father-substitute or father-symbol, or indeed any source of authority which is feared or dreaded, can suffice. Sometimes perhaps unwittingly we generate in young people an attitude of negativism by setting up the wrong emotional currents, so that while their intellect and will are with us, their behavior is the opposite of what we and even they themselves desire. It is almost a case of *Video meliora, proboque, deteriora sequor*. Many have been confronted with the widespread phenomenon of the young person who in her own words "cannot get on with her mother, or her father, or her teacher" etc. There is very often in this sort of case, a deep and genuine mutual love, together with inability to express it, or to act in accordance with it, and this inability is due to emotional factors. Such negativism on the part of the child is a reflection of the parent's or teacher's attitude. The parent very often thinks he will achieve his purpose by telling the child what to do. But he has no real confidence that the child will in fact do what he tells him. The child in turn hears the instruction, but "feels" the lack of confidence, by a process called empathy, and it is this which determines both his attitude and his behavior. In general, I suggest, children and adolescents behave much more in accordance with what they think we expect of them than in accordance with what we tell them to do. This parental situation is imported into the school, especially in matters of religious practice. We generate a mental revolt by coloring our instruction with the wrong affective tone, through lack of real confidence that they will rise to the level of our aspiration for them.

The greatest difficulty in the problem of religion and
mental health is to keep the distinction between the natural
and the supernatural orders clear. The difficulty derives from
the fact that the supernatural permeates the natural in so
many ways; that we ourselves are not departmentalized but
live a natural and supernatural life as one person at one and
the same time; that our prayer is so often for temporal objects; that we use natural means in teaching religion; that we
are sometimes not at all clear about the distinction between
the will of God as manifested through secondary causes, and
direct divine intervention. Thus the typical malaise and
acute insecurity of the adolescent is not automatically "cured"
by prayer. Nor is the typical anxiety of middle age necessarily a "spiritual" trial. Both these conditions are due to
natural causes: the one to the threefold conflict between
physiological, emotional and intellectual maturation which
proceed at different rates; the other to the awareness of de-
clining powers, the sense of failure or futility, and the difficulty of adjusting to a new tempo of life. More marked still,
because more often seemingly religious in character, is the
condition of the late fifties called involutional melancholia—
a condition characterized by an unbearable sense of guilt
and repudiation. This condition is probably precipitated,
or at any rate contributed to, by the fear of death, and once
again is a natural illness.

In these three typical conditions, weird and frightening
mental contents will appear, welling up from the deep unconscious, or more simply, the irrational side of man's nature
will become painfully obtrusive. But though guilt, sin, temptation, Heaven and Hell may play obvious and important
parts in the mental life of an individual suffering in that
way, we are not yet in the presence of a religious problem.
It is inevitable that what has been or has appeared to be of

very great importance in one's normal healthy life, will appear at the focus of a disturbed thought process; and since religious belief and practice are at once the most important and the most fearful elements in human life, it is clear that they will play an important part in any neurotic (or psychotic) condition. Undoubtedly, any natural misfortune or suffering can be used to advantage by the believing Christian: *omnia cooperantur in bonum.* But a natural misfortune or suffering is not of itself a spiritual trial. I am inclined to stress this because all too often these natural ills of mental life have been represented either to or by the sufferer as straight spiritual trials, whereas in such conditions spiritual effort may only aggravate the condition. It is important to remember that neurotic symptoms of a compulsive character may be aggravated rather than cured by having recourse to repetitive or vocal prayer, for example. It is also of the first importance to note that the emotional guilt of the adolescent, the middle-aged anxiety state and the involutional condition have little if anything to do with strict theological guilt for sin. The latter is rational judgment that one has done something, *sciens volens,* and that it was morally wrong. The guilt-feeling of the neurotic, on the other hand, is an emotional state composed of many elements among which we can distinguish fear, self-loathing, hatred, etc.

Thus it becomes tremendously important to distinguish properly between "scruples" in the strict theological sense, and neurotic compulsive behavior. Both of these in turn should be distinguished from the normal fear and dread of sin. The scrupulous person is going through a spiritual trial which, properly used, can advance him on the spiritual plane, whereas the neurotic is, by the very nature of his neurosis and to the degree of its severity, handicapped in all that respects voluntary and therefore meritorious action. The individual who cannot get through the Rosary because he must repeat each Hail Mary until he is satisfied, is not scrupulous but sick. But the person whose conscience is troubled by each smallest imperfection as though it were mortal sin, may be genuinely scrupulous but mentally very healthy indeed. The simplest test I can think of is to look for the motive. If the motive is fear, or pride, or if one can be reasonably sure that greater and more serious matters are being ignored, one can assume either an unhealthy mental condition or straight malingering, whereas if the motive is a noble one and the rest of the personality is fairly well integrated, one may suspect a genuine case of scruples. Even here, however, one should be loath to acknowledge a genuine spritual problem to the exclusion of a natural one, and especially one should be careful not to let adolescents get hold of the idea too easily that they are "scrupulous". Very often a little more care in the examination of conscience would do them all the good in the world.

I sometimes think that in matters of religion we are in danger of committing the Platonic fallacy—the theory that if people know the good, they will automatically do it. It is true if people do not know the good, or the right, it will be very difficult for them to do it. "How can they hear unless it be preached to them?" But it is certainly not true that mere knowledge will of itself bring about good behavior. Very often it is not knowledge, the cognitive side of mental life, which most directly influences our behavior, but the conative side: the emotions, appetites, desires, in short, concupiscence. Undoubtedly, knowledge must be given, especially in matters of the sixth commandment. But equally what cannot be given is any adequate notion of the impact of desire on consciousness and therefore on behavior. The knowledge we impart may in fact have as one of its results the stimulating of curiosity, and thereby the awakening of desire. All the knowledge in the world will not of itself eliminate or counteract the force of desire. Clearly the adolescent or young adult should be prepared for this challenge, but equally clearly no one but himself can do anything about it when it arises. Knowledge does not allay concupiscence nor does grace eliminate desire.

On the other hand one should not assume, as many contemporary psychologists and moralists would seem to assume, that if one behaves in ways that conflict with the state and degree of one's knowledge, therefore there is something wrong with one's mental health. This is simply not so. It is precisely because one can so behave that moral behavior is possible—that is, that man is a free and responsible agent. Looking at the matter realistically, therefore, it is only to be expected (but that does not mean condoned or excused) that behavior will at least sometimes not measure up to the degree of knowledge possessed, or again that some people will behave in unexpected ways in direct conflict with the instruction given or the standards set for them. If this were not so we would not be dealing with human beings. It is sometimes apparent that people enjoy being scandalized by the deviant behavior of others—even, be it said, that they sometimes achieve a sort of vicarious satisfaction in contemplating and recounting the deeds of others. In this sort of case—one hesitates to say it—the unhealthy thinking is their own.

One last point: does our actual instruction in religion sometimes lead to unhealthy ways of thinking and acting? Consider for instance the simple error of telling children that their souls are really little angels, that after death they become little angels, and so on. This is probably harmless in the vast majority of cases. But it does introduce a dichotomy into human nature which can sometimes produce severe conflict later on: the sort of conflict which reaches theological proportions in Manichaeism, Albigensianism, and all forms of extreme repudiation of matter or the organism. This may sound an exaggeration, but one certainly finds adolescents and young adults who are unable emotionally or psychologically to accept their own human nature in its fullness. Again, we are not always sufficiently careful in our teaching about sin, guilt and punishment. The notion of sin is in itself sufficiently terrible not to need a charge of emotional horror on our part to bring it home to children. Emotional horror, fear, dread, anxiety, generate not an awareness of responsibility for wrong-doing, but guilt in the psychiatrist's sense: neurotic guilt, an unhealthy state of the emotions and by no means necessarily a salutary experience. In treating of the punishment of sin, we sometimes at least give the impression that retribution follows even in this life. The evils and misfortunes which befall people are the will of God punishing people for their sins. There is no doubt that this can be interpreted in a perfectly sound theological sense, but neither is there any doubt that it is very difficult to do so accurately. To the children's mind, on the other hand, it is very often a purely literal and anthropomorphic operation.

Fortunately, the mind, like the body, has its own ways of dealing with some at least of its unhealthy conditions, so that the vast majority of people grow to maturity without meeting any of the dire problems I have been considering. But there are always the few who suffer very much, and with the apparent increase in neurotic conditions, or perhaps the decrease in the ability to rectify these conditions from within the individual himself, I think it behooves us wherever possible to lessen the precipitating causes. Prophylaxis is always better than treatment.

2 oedipus complex and anima rationalis

"Traditional psychology", under which term I include both the "great" systems of philosophical psychology, and the more recent "classics" of empirical psychology, has always been structural in outlook, i.e., it has attempted to state what the mind is, while analytic theory, and a few recent works in experimental psychology, have been "functional" in character, i.e., they have attempted to show what the mind does, or how it works. The contrast can be brought out in many ways. Compare for instance, the analytic conception of the topography of the mind with the traditional "structural" picture:

Conscious,
Preconscious,
Subconscious,
Unconscious,
}
Considered as "Regions
of the Psyche";

Intellect and will,
Internal and External Senses,
Emotions,
Instincts,
}
Considered as faculties
of the mind.

In the first list, the interplay of cognitive and affective factors is taken for granted, but the question of the origin and nature of these factors is largely untouched. In the second list, the psychologist is preoccupied with the detailed examination of the different capacities listed, while their interplay and consequences in the unity of the human mind and the molding of personality are very often ignored.

The contrast can be seen in more detail by a comparison of Freud's psychodynamics of forgetting (repression due to the affective-tone of the "forgotten" item—see *Psychopathology of Everyday Life*) with studies of the "curve of forgetting" in any psychology manual. The analytic concept is that nothing is ever really forgotten, but that some cognitive contents become inaccessible. They are described as being "in the Unconscious", existing "dynamically", and functioning in such a way that their effects are discernible, e.g., in dreams, or even in waking life in the form of compulsions, hysterias, anxieties, etc. Analytic theory is not interested in rates of forgetting, disturbances of the curve due to "reminiscence", retroactive inhibition, the alleged variation of retentive capacity with age, the merits of "whole" versus "part" learning as measured in terms of what is retained and what is forgotten, and other phenomena of this order. In a word, analytic psychology has no theory of memory. In this, it is not alone. The same contrast between structural and functional psychology can be brought out by contrasting the work of Ebbinghaus (*Uber das Gedächtniss*, 1855) with Sir Frederick Bartlett's work (*Remembering*, 1932). In fact, the contrast could hardly be better shown than by Bartlett's own examination of it in his first chapter. For Ebbinghaus, memory was as it were a self-contained, self-regulating mechanism, subject to its own laws, capable of being studied in isolation, and explained from within itself. Bartlett, who is anything but an analyst, studies re-membering as a function of the whole man in which the serial reproduction of acquired cognitive material or of organ-ized sequences of bodily movement plays little or no part. It is a function which involves the cooperation of what in a different terminology would be called intellect, sensory ca-pacities and emotions.

By means of a series of ingenious experiments, Bartlett brings out the complexities of remembering "at the human level", and on the basis of his experiments, he puts forward a theory of remembering whose merits have escaped the notice of many psychologists. There are many reasons for this. Bartlett, like the analysts, has no theory on memory: "It is perfectly true that nobody can set a ring around Memory and explain it from within itself. The dissolving power of modern research seems to have split Memory into a number of variously related functions." He is, therefore, at variance with the traditional structuralists. Secondly, by implication at least, Bartlett has abandoned the sensist ver-sion of human cognition and the mechanist interpretation of stimulus and response in human behavior. The third reason is more subtle, perhaps. The theory is a very difficult one to appreciate properly, and this, combined with its clear break with the sensist-associationist tradition has generated re-sistance to its acceptance.

There is another crucial point on which the "functional" experimentalists and the analysts agree. In Bartlett's words: "The psychologist, whether he uses experimental methods or not, is dealing, not simply with reactions but with human beings." With this principle also, the traditional "philosophi-cal" psychologists, whether scholastic or not, are in agree-ment. It is often forgotten in practice, however, both by the traditional structuralists, and by the stimulus-response school of experimentalists, both of whom, by studying a process in isolation as though it were a closed circuit or a self-contained mechanism, get the whole man out of focus.

It is precisely on this fundamental principle that analytic theory has staked its claim to acceptance. It claims to be a theory of human nature, of personality, of the normal and the abnormal mind; and it is on this basis that it must be evaluated, not in terms of whether or not particular matters of detail happen to be correct or not.

It is inherently unlikely, or even impossible, as any student of the logic of science will know, that any particular scientific theory constitutes the last word on its subject, or attains the level of final and complete explanation. And analytic theory claims at any rate to be a scientific theory of man. More to the point perhaps are the words of the late Dr. H. Stack Sullivan, one of the most stimulating analytic theorists that America has produced: "The human mind did not cease to think with the death of Freud." In other words, in spite of the extravagances of some analysts in proclaiming the *ipse dixit* of the master (even of his contradictory doctrines at different times), it is becoming more and more widely accepted that the specific teachings of Freud himself are not the last word on man. In the same way, perhaps, the doctrines of the nuclear physicists are not the last word on the universe. But he would be a rash scientist indeed who rejected them on these grounds. Equally rash, in my opinion, would be the psychologist or philosopher who rejected the analytic doctrines on the ground of their incompleteness or lack of finality. Nuttin is careful to point out that it is no longer possible for the scientific student of human nature to reject analytic theory out of hand, nor as a scientist to accept it all uncritically.

It is of course arguable, as Broad once pointed out, that

the doctrines of the "depth-psychologists or analysts were well known for centuries to priests, poets and philosophers. But if they were, they were known more in the form of intuitive understandings of human beings than in the form of scientific "insights" into human nature on an empirical, experimental, and clinical basis, which would serve in turn for the erection of far-reaching theories.

Any critical approach to these far-reaching theories must meet certain philosophical and/or semantic difficulties at the very outset. These are the difficulties inherent in such general conceptions as "mental-mechanisms", "psychic energy", and "regions" of the mind, and in the more particular and determinate conceptions indicated by "conflict", "repression", "conversion" (of a mental content or process into a physical symptom), to list only a few of them. If these are taken literally, quite obviously they are materialist-mechanist conceptions, and cannot apply in their ordinary physical significance to the non-material reality called mind. This factor constituted and still constitutes a major difficulty not only for what Nuttin calls "the spiritualist" conception of man, but also for the non-spiritualist but philosophico-humanist-rationalist view of man. But if on the other hand they are not taken literally, the semantic difficulty arises: they appear in practice to describe something, but what exactly do they describe?

The important thing here is to try to understand what exactly analytic theory intends by such conceptions, instead of trying to score a quick but pyrrhic victory over the analysts in the tradition of some philosophy manuals by referring to the *opiniones insanae adversariorum*. For in what follows, I am not concerned with whether or not Freud, Rank, Stekel, Adler, etc., were materialists or hedonists or mechanists, nor am I concerned with what individual authors and practitioners may have said, but rather with the question whether analytic theory *in globo* has the kind of merit which any scientific theory at a particular point in the history of science might be presumed to have.

There is a further preliminary consideration. It is true that the value of analysis (the therapeutic use of analytic theory) has not been established by any statistical assessment of results, such as is available in the case of most major therapeutic procedures used for physical disorders. It is also true that prolonged "deep" analysis as a major psychotherapeutic means is falling more and more into disfavor with the majority of psychiatrists and has become the prerogative of the (comparatively) small number of "orthodox" psycho-analysts. True, again, that many of the "apparent" cures after two or three (or sometimes as many as seven) years' analysis might be due to spontaneous remissions, or recovery through the combination of maturation and the simple passage of time. But these are criticisms of analysis, not of analytic theory, i.e., of the procedure of the analyst, not of the analyst's conception of human nature. In this context also it should be pointed out, as was stated at the outset, that the method of analysis is not necessarily linked, either logically or psychologically, with the theory of any particular school of psychology, Freudian or otherwise, though the majority of analysts think it is. For the method of analysis, when it is successful, effects its cure either by abreaction or by catharsis. By the former is meant precipitating, and thereby releasing, a more or less violent emotional reaction. The emotion, through being pent up like steam in a boiler above the maximum pressure for safety, is thought of as seeking an outlet, and cannot find the safety valve. (This analogy, based on the fact of abreaction, is the source of the theory of emotionally charged ideas or images "existing dynamically" in their own right "in the unconscious". The alternative procedure of catharsis consists in taking out into the open and facing in cold blood, as it were, the noisome and repulsive idea (or "memory") of an "experience" (or "wish", etc.) which consciousness refuses to face. Both abreaction and catharsis can be used independently of any "theory", and indeed even independently of analytic method, as is done for instance in some recent developments of narcotherapy.

It is very tempting to point out some of the philosophical absurdities in analytic theory, and this has been done many times. It is too often forgotten, however, that the analytic theorists were not philosophers, any more than the average man in the street. Pointing out these philosophical errors is just about as profitable as pointing out the astronomical absurdities involved in saying the sun rises in the east and sets in the west. This latter phrase describes a phenomenon, and does so well enough to enable us to tell the time, to find our way, and to do a host of other things. These are also the purposes of analytic theory—it is empirical in source and intention. Besides, just as one can point to certain philosophical absurdities in analytic theory, so also can one point to certain philosophical absurdities in the popular "spiritualist" view of man. This latter, so far from giving an adequate conception of the union of a spiritual principle with matter, is very often either a carry-over of the Platonic View, so severely dealt with by St. Thomas, or an unrecognized version of the Cartesian dualism which is responsible both for subjective idealism, empiricism, and mechanism.

This must not be taken to mean that philosophical criticism is irrelevant, but only that it very often misses the point. The counterpart of this on the analytic side is the equally absurd and facile presumption that analytic theory demands a remolding of the concept of man and the construction of a new moral code (e.g., in Flugel's *Man, Morals and Society,* 1945).

The responsibility for the popular misconceptions of what analytic theories are about rests with three groups—the analysts themselves, who with the enthusiasm of neophytes exaggerate the importance of their new instruments and conceptions, and were not philosophers, though they were dealing with a philosophy of human nature; the "popularizers," who saw the possibility of "selling" psychology in the same way as detective fiction and pornography; and the public at large, whose appetite grew by what it fed on. For the popular version is that psychoanalysis and analytic theory are "all about sex", which is not true even of orthodox thoroughgoing Freudianism. It is generally recognized both inside and outside the analytic circle, that the term sex in the pansexual context of analytic theory, is a technical term, not to be equated with the colloquial use of the same word. (In this connection the section on psychoanalysis in Fr. Bonnar's *The Catholic Doctor* might be profitably consulted.)

The more obvious statements of analytic theory can be taken as read, and also the more obvious points of criticism. The essential points from the theory however are very often missed. These can best be understood perhaps if we preface them by a series of negative statements. Analytic theory is not a theory of the soul, nor of the mind, nor of the relation of body and mind. It is not a denial of spirit, nor of intellect and will, nor of the moral law. It is not a doctrine of license or libertinism, nor a denial of free will and grace. Finally, it is not a doctrine of hedonism nor an epicurean philosophy. In fact, it is not philosophy. And these statements hold in spite of the express pronouncements of Freud and others which might be quoted substantiating each of the propositions I have denied. Freud thought of religion as a neurosis

—but Jung emphatically did not. Freud thought the libido the only and sufficient source of energy and impulse to account for the whole complex of human endeavor—but Adler most emphatically did not. Freud and others thought along deterministic and materialistic lines—but Bartemeier, President of the International Institute of Psycho-Analysis, 1950, certainly does not. And so on through the whole list— one author can be quoted against another all the way. That is why I say analytic theory is none of these things, while each and all of them may be all theories of individual analysts.

Analytic theory is a body of doctrine concerning (a) the nature and dynamics of certain kinds of mental content, (b) some of the processes which go on in every mind, normal and abnormal, and (c) the genesis of certain conditions (which may be either psychical of physical or both) which are symptomatic of the unhealthy functioning of the process listed under (b). These doctrines are expressed in figurative language, and in analogical and empirical terminology. The figurative language is not really misleading if its source is understood, though the scientific mind may find it repulsive. But the analogical use of concepts from the physical sciences (in the first instance as descriptive, but then taken to be explanatory) can be misleading. As descriptive, they come under the head of "saving the appearance", but as explanatory they cease to be scientific or psychological.

There are two kinds of cognitive content—intellectual and sensory. One of the great *lacunae* in analytic theory is that it takes account only of the sensory, i.e., sense-experience and its derivative imagery. But to its credit, analytic theory has thrown some light on these aspects of human cognition. The terminology which makes "the Unconscious" the "abode" of experience unknown to introspection is merely descriptive.

But the fact described is very real. It is true, in other words, that some of the results of sensory experience are not at the moment retrievable by voluntary effort. In ordinary language, they are not just "forgotten", as the former group might be described. They are such that we never even knew we had them. It would be rash to discount the clinical evidence that such items are recoverable, either under hypnosis, or by "free association", or by dream analysis. Undoubtedly, the apparent recovery of such items is sometimes not a case of remembering through analysis, but is a simple inferential process, suggested by the analyst, in which the patient cooperates, and which is describable as an answer to the question: What must have been the case in infancy in order that such and such a phenomenon now apparent should have been produced? It is, in other words, a simple argument *a posteriori* from effect to cause. In this case, the cause postulated can very well be regarded as a postulate depending on the analyst's theoretical formulations. But there are still many cases attested by the patients themselves wherein the "lost" item is recovered spontaneously under analysis.

The whole notion of "regions" of the psyche can very well be dispensed with without loss to analytic theory, and for it can be substituted the concept of "degree of accessibility" of cognitive content. This brings the Freudian unconscious much closer to the Thomistic concept of "habitual knowledge" (the way in which memory can be attributed to the intellect) and to the phantasia (some of whose processes were already known to be unconscious, e.g., the preparation of the sense data for the process of abstraction) and the (not necessarily) introspectible process of *conversio ad phantasmata* in the knowledge of singulars.

With regard to the dynamics of imagery, the point stressed by analytic theory is that images remain active, affecting

conscious contents and overt behavior, while they themselves can be unconscious. This is due to the fact that they
are heavily charged with emotion. For "image" the analyst
very often uses the term "idea", so that a "complex" is definable as a repressed idea with attested fact, both empirically
and experimentally, but the fact that consciousness can unconsciously repudiate a particular image because of its ex-
ceedingly unpleasant emotional tone (and thereby "forget"
it) is one which might well have escaped attention were it
not for the findings of analysis. The terminology of repression,
complex, the unconscious and the threshold or "censor"
between the unconscious and consciousness is not necessary,
but what it describes is a fact.

Among the processes which go on in every mind, normal
and abnormal, are those of introjection, projection, repression, and sublimation, to name only a few. The essential
points here are that the analyst is describing in a picturesque
way some of the aspects of human reactions to a complex
environment, and secondly, that it is not the process, but its
content which is distorted in the neurotic or pscho-neurotic.
The human being in infancy is a *tabula rasa,* and must acquire all his subsequently discernible mental content. This
he does by contact with people and things. In terms of the
emotional charge of cognitive content, the most telling experiences in infancy will be those concerned with the people
who mean most for the infant's emotional life—mother,
father, and siblings, in that order.

The term infantile sexuality means simply the diffused
organic pleasure (or the "quiescence of the organism") con-
sequent upon the satisfaction of any bodily need. A high
pleasure-tone means that the child will seek the exciting
cause again, while an unpleasant experience will be avoided.
Thorndike's "Law of Effect" in the learning-process is very

close to the analyst's conception here. The avoiding of the repetition of an unpleasant experience is the result of the emotional charge of the repressed memory of the first experience of similar emotional tone. But where the analyst helps is in the consequence of this concept. The unpleasant emotion associated with the repressed item can be split off (dissociated) from the original item, and linked with a different image or idea, or the original image can be represented in consciousness by a substitute resembling it in some way, however tenuous and vague, called by the analysts a "symbol". From now on, this second image is dreaded and repudiated, or the dissociated emotion now joined with it affects behavior in such a way as to produce neurotic symptoms, while the symbol, on the other hand, may be accepted by consciousness because of the loss of the emotional charge, or may affect behavior in other ways.

The process of introjection describes in a picturesque way the process whereby the child, long before it can formulate rational and objective judgments of right and wrong, learns to "behave properly" and "be a good child". Once more, the fact described is clear, while the analyst's description of it ("the introjection of the father-figure and generation of the super-ego") can be misleading or even repulsive. Projection is again the familiar fact that the child will say (or will learn from his mother to say) "naughty chair" when he barks his shin, or the adult, feeling over-anxious or dyspeptic, will blame his staff for his own inadequacies. These processes are universal, and help one to understand any mind, normal or abnormal.

Under the third head (genesis of symptoms) comes the most fruitful contribution of analytic theory to the study of human nature. That imagery and emotion played some part in the production of bodily disorders was long ago well known. In this context it is possible to quote St. Thomas Aquinas: *Medici dicunt esse intendendum somniis ad cognoscendum interiores dispositiones* (S. Theol., 2-2,95,6). In the aetiology of mental disturbance the role of imagery and emotion was even more widely accepted. But it remained for the analyst to produce a theory as to how bodily and mental disorders were brought about by emotional and cognitional factors, and to show how much disorders might be cured.

Out of this section of analytic theory come the now universally accepted accounts of conversion hysteria, anxiety-neurosis, psychosomatic disorders and so on. The analytic theory depends on the concept of "conflict"—the struggle of a repressed item seeking release, or of an impulse or instinct seeking fulfillment, on the one hand, with the repressing forces of the super-ego (or consciousness, or morality, or social taboos) on the other. The physical symptom is conceived either as the translation of a repressed psychical item into a physical one, or as the physical effect of a psychical cause. Here again, a fact vouched for by clinical experience is being described. A more scientifically exact, and certainly a more philosophically acceptable account of the same phenomena can readily enough be formulated in terms not of psychical and physical systems interacting, but in terms of the psychophysical composite nature of man as one being, not two accidentally linked together. But since the "cure" depends ultimately on giving the patient himself some degree of insight into his condition, the simplified "descriptive" version of analytic theory seems to be warranted in practice. It would be much more difficult to explain to a patient the functions of the parasympathetic nervous system and the endocrine glands as integral components of an emotional state and not merely consequential or antecedent phenomena, than to explain to him that he "feels anxious" and this produces the "sinking feeling" which, protracted through a long time-process, can in turn produce a peptic ulcer.

It is worth noting in passing that the dualism implied in analytic theory (not explicitly accepted by many analysts though they talk in terms of it) is the Cartesian dualism of mind (a "thinking thing") united to matter (something extended), while the nature of the cure can be stated in Platonic terms as giving back to the pilot the control of the ship. In other words, where reason was at the mercy of the non-rational element (imagery and emotions) the analyst, by giving the patient an understanding of his condition, tries to place reason in control again. That, as I understand it, is the whole aim and purpose of psychotherapy of any kind.

The notion that the analyst or therapist seeks only to remove controls and lead his patient to license is negatived even by Freud himself, who claims that some degree of "repression" is necessary for mental health. The concept of sublimation also implies that a human being must not remain the plaything of impulse and instinct. The fact described by sublimation is the obvious one that man can strive for objectives appropriate to the human level, as well as for those more closely correlated with his animal nature.

It will be seen from the foregoing that the essential concepts of analytic theory harmonize readily enough with the traditional concept of human nature implied in western philosophy. But it is important to note that this harmony is discernible only on condition that both analytic theory and human nature are adequately understood. The idea that man is an angel accidentally imprisoned for a time in the prison-house of the flesh is not a correct idea of man, and, as such, conflicts with the findings of analytic work. The idea that religion is a neurosis is not part of the content of analytic theory, and conflicts with the proper concept of man. The picturesque idea of the analyst that every man is abnormal—"there is no such thing as the normal mind"—must be properly understood. It means simply that the mental processes of maladjusted and of well-adjusted people are the same, the difference being one of degree and content.

Apart from the illumination of non-introspectible mental processes, there are three further ways in which analytic theory helps in understanding human nature. It gives us some clue as to why this particular person has the kind of personality he has; it underlines the enormously complex structure of human motivation at all levels; and it restores the "animal" part of the definition of man, which the rationalist conception of him tended to ignore. It was Freud's idea that the first few years of life, but especially the emotional relationship between son and mother, daughter and father, had a final and determining effect on the subsequent personality. The *oedipus complex* and all that it implies has passed into the daily language of most people, and it would be rash to think that it is devoid of foundation. But it has been radically altered from Freud's own version, through Jung, Horney, Rank, Sullivan, and others. The chief alteration in the theory is the abandonment of the ineradicability or ultimately determining efficacy of infantile experience. This is particularly noteworthy in the Group for the Advancement of Psychiatry in America, and the pronouncements of the World Federation for Mental Health.

Are there, then, any defects in analytic theory? There are, and they are legion. But they have been so often stressed, that perhaps a brief summary of them here will suffice. Analytic theory has no concept of spirit, in spite of Jung's *Modern Man in Search of a Soul*. It has no adequate concept of the nature and role of intellect, and it denies (though very often only verbally) the existence of will, while in practice its method of cure, as we saw, consists in restoring intellect and will to their proper place. It is not an internally consistent theory, and its inconsistencies are not often acknowledged. It is often uncritical (or rather Freud was often uncritical) in the kind of evidence used to substantiate an hypothesis, and hypotheses are not scientifically validated by testing them against their predictable consequences. Finally, it has often been pointed out that orthodox psychoanalysts and their teachings are sometimes unscientific inasmuch as they seem to believe that what Freud has said is the truth for the psychoanalyst, and if he has said contradictory things, the fault rests with the person who cannot accept contradictions.

But in spite of all that, it is still true that analytic theory has come to stay. Freud's trick of inventing a mythology, instead of constructing a scientific terminology, to describe the phenomena he studied should not blind us to the fact that he did study phenomena and not myths. It is the task of the structural psychologist now to give a functional description of his phenomena, using the help of analytic insights, and so produce an integral empirical and rational psychology of man.

3 the adolescent

Human life moves in a sequence of phases, more or less well-defined, each of which presents its own special characteristics, problems, and advantages. These phases, for our purposes, can be listed as follows: infancy, childhood, adolescence, conscious adulthood, marriage and parenthood, final maturity, and senescence. Some of these phases are easily definable, for example, infancy and childhood, marriage and parenthood. But the others are more complicated.

I use the phrase "conscious adulthood" for instance, because adulthood is not necessarily reached at the age of twenty-one. This is legal adulthood. But a man is not really an adult until he has reached the conscious awareness that he is now an independent entity, bearing a tremendous responsibility, standing alone in his own right as a person. Again, senescence is not an easy phase to define. It is not the same as senility. It simply means growing old. It refers to the phase which follows the full realization and maturity of one's powers, and can begin almost at any time from the middle thirties. Usually however, it begins in the fifties.

Now, as far as development of personality is concerned, all these phases are important. They are in fact the critical points in life where the human person is most susceptible to influences for good or ill. They are the crucial points where if desirable influences are brought to bear on the individual, they can have their most telling effect, and where undesirable influences can have their most devastating effect. And of all these phases, adolescence is the most important.

The period of adolescence is also the most mysterious in life. It is a curious transition stage, a mixture of realization and unfulfilled promise, of the fantasy world of childhood and the real world of the adult. It comes on suddenly, and vanishes as it were overnight. Even though we have all been through it, we shall never fully understand it, since there is no re-entry. We have even forgotten and cannot now recapture our own adolescence, and tend in spite of ourselves to expect the adolescent to see the world through our adult eyes, where the most we can do really is to prepare him to see it eventually through his own eyes when the time comes.

The clue to adolescence lies in the concept of maturation. The human being goes through a constant process of change and development all through life. But he does not develop in all respects at the same time, nor in the same way, nor at the same rate. For our purposes, I draw attention to a three-fold maturation which will help towards the understanding of the adolescent—physical, intellectual, and emotional maturation.

Physical maturation refers to the growth of the organism, and specifically to the process whereby the organism attains the capacity of self-production. This is what we mean by puberty, the complicated organic changes which take place in the teens—in the case of boys a year or so later than in the case of girls—and which are a remote preparation for parenthood. There is quite a considerable variation in age in some individuals, and one can only give average figures. In general, in the vast majority of cases this first kind of

maturity is attained in the early teens. When I call it physical maturity, of course, this does not imply that physically
the organism does not develop after this point. Of course it
does. This is one kind of physical maturation, or one stage
in physical maturation.

The problem of the adolescent might conceivably be
much simpler if he matured in other respects at the same
rate as his physical development. But this is not so. The
child begins to use his reason at a very early stage in life.
At first this is a groping uncertain operation. By the age of
seven he is usually spoken of as having attained the use of
reason, but this is still a far cry from the full development
of his intellectual capacity. But this development goes forward at an increasing rate into the teens, and the individual
normally reaches his peak of intellectual capacity at about
fifteen. Let us be a little bit conservative and put it at sixteen.
Notice that I have spoken of intellectual capacity rather than
attainment, because of course he will not have attained his
full intellectual content by that time. But his capacity to
receive and absorb knowledge or mental content will never,
as a rule, be any greater than it is at sixteen. This is our
second maturation point, the process of intellectual maturation.

But it is the third maturation process which really com-
plicates the whole picture, the process of emotional maturation.

The emotional life of the child is comparatively simple.
He responds with pleasant feelings to pleasant things; he
answers affection with affection. He manifests his likes and
dislikes simply and directly, knowing instinctively as it were
that his emotional outbursts will serve to rid himself of unpleasant experiences, and to ensure the satisfaction of his

wants. He does not reflect on his emotional states, for he cannot, and so they are not a puzzle for him.

But with the onset of puberty, the capacity for emotional experience is vastly expanded. The emotions go deeper in intensity, are more varied in quality, more extensive in sheer quantity. And remember that the intellect is going ahead by leaps and bounds just at this time. Curiosity, a desire for knowledge, is aroused. Self-consciousness, in the sense of consciousness of self, becomes acute, the capacity for reflection and self-analysis develops, so that intellect is confronted with a new set of rather bewildering problems. But it has a long way to go yet before it can even begin to understand the nature of these emotional processes. Emotional maturity is for the majority of people the last of the three to be achieved—and some peple, let us admit, never achieve it at all.

Because of the maturation of the organism, the expanded capacity for emotional experience, and the bewilderment of a growing intellect with a corresponding growth in understanding, the adolescent very often becomes aware of a vague uneasiness, a feeling of malaise, or anxiety, which he cannot explain to himself. There are many causes for this anxiety. There is perhaps a reluctance to "put away the things of a child"—to forsake the secure world of childhood, and face the rather incomprehensible world of the adult. Part of this is undoubtedly the fear of the unknown, part also the fear of responsibility—in general, the fear of growing up. And the oddest part of it is that growing up is also attractive. The adolescent is no longer a child, and not yet a man. And yet he is still a child in many ways, and already a man in some respects. It is this conflict which accounts for a great deal of the conflicting emotions of the adolescent, and for the ensuing bewilderment. This vague anxiety, coupled with the growth in physical capacity and emotional life leads very often to hyperactivity in the case of boys, and the typical tantrums or hysteria in girls.

But there are other components of the restlessness or uneasiness of the adolescent. Adolescence is the time when talents emerge, often unsuspected up to then. They are as yet undeveloped, mere potentialities, which seek fulfillment, and the boy very often does not know what to do with them, or about them. His energy and enthusiasm run high, and generosity and goodwill are at their peak. All these factors combined give rise to the typical idealism and romanticism of adolescence. Never again in the course of his life will the boy be as ready to accept a worthwhile ideal to strive for as at this point in his development. Later on, cynicism and disillusionment together with the pain of life will have taken their toll. But now these forces play no part. A certain amount of romanticism, expressed in daydreams or fantasy, is typical of this phase. The adolescent sees himself in the part of whoever happens to be his hero for the time being—the popular footballer, film star, or spaceship ranger—or in a private world of his own he carries out exploits of daredeviltry and heroism by imitating in play the exciting exploits of real life. All this, within reason, is good and healthy. But the phrase "within reason" is the nub of the matter, for although the adolescent has attained the use of reason several years earlier, he will nevertheless not see himself or judge his actions according to the mature reason of the adult. It would be a mistake to expect him to do so. And that is why supervision, a gentle restraint, and wise discipline are indispensable.

The adolescent needs constant advice and training in maxims of good behavior. But he does not always, or even often, accept, as an adult might, an abstract principle, and proceed to apply it as a standard of judgment to the present concrete situation. That comes later. The adolescent takes a shortcut in determining how he ought to behave. This he accomplishes through the twin processes of identification and imitation. Hero-worship is the most natural thing in the world for the adolescent. He selects his hero, identifies himself in imagination with him, and imitates (consciously or unconsciously) his behavior. You may see this carried to absurd lengths, by adult standards, when the adolescent imitates the walk, the speech, even the hair-style of his hero, as well as his standards of behavior. What should the adult do when he finds himself the object of such hero-worship? Not, I suggest, repudiate it summarily, but make himself worthy of it. Above all, he should never, even in small things, present a pattern for the adolescent to imitate, of which he should be ashamed.

Man is a social animal—not simply a gregarious animal. Gregarious animals congregate together and travel in packs for purposes of mutual defense and food-seeking. But man is not just an animal. He is a reasonable creature with an immortal soul. And it was part of the Divine Plan for man that he should live with his fellowmen in groups, in order that each member might contribute something to the formation of his fellows. The full flowering of each man's personality is only possible in the interplay and complicated relations of human society. The tendency which leads ultimately to the formation of the state as we know it in the modern world has its roots very deep indeed in human nature. And the period of adolescence is the point at which this need for group structure or organization makes itself felt for the first time. The adolescent very often has difficulty in making the various adjustments which are called for in social relations, due to self-consciousness, uneasiness, or even simple physical awkwardness. And yet he needs and feels the need of the society of his fellows. He needs to have the sharp corners of his personality smoothed and this is done in association with others. If he fails outright in this (and some few do in fact fail) he may develop into a shy, shut-in, maladjusted, rather unlovable type of person; or he may become the kind of person who seems to be always suffering from a sense of grievance, the kind of person which popular magazines sometimes refer to as anti-social.

But this innate tendency towards social organization has a further interest and importance for us. It is quite certain that any group of adolescents for whom no group-structure or organization is provided will inevitably provide one for themselves. This can take any one of a thousand forms. But unfortunately, in our urban civilization, it almost invariably takes the form of the "gang". The "gang" organization is obviously not in itself a bad thing, since it springs from an innate disposition which is good. But the trouble arises out of a second factor, equally inevitable. An organization of human beings which has no purpose cannot survive for long. Now it happens very often that a group of adolescents, following their natural inclination, form a gang. And then they find that they have nothing to do—perhaps for the simple reason that they have no equipment for games and no money to buy any. The next stage is easy. They must discover some purpose to hold the gang together, or else break up. They will not normally break up voluntarily and so they choose a purpose. The purpose so chosen, without adult guidance, and without means or equipment or understanding, can sometimes be a nefarious one. If you add to all these facts the fact mentioned already of the tendency to imitation, you can see how a group of youngsters can easily move without malice aforethought from the stage of being a gang to the stage of being gangsters.

When a human being is one of a group, he will very often behave differently from the way in which he would behave if he were entirely on his own. This is due to many factors, the chief one being the fact that the consciousness of individual responsibility is submerged in the collective emotional drive of the group. One of the causes of juvenile delinquency is undoubtedly to be found in the combination of the various factors just listed: the innate tendency towards group activity the forming of the purposeless gang, and the diminution of responsibility in the sense indicated. There are of course many factors involved: one must never forget the doctrine of original sin, and the fact that the irrational side of man's nature is not wholly under the control of reason. And, because original sin is a factor involved here, neither should one forget the efficacy of Grace.

I have mentioned certain critical points in human development where the individual is most susceptible to influences for good or ill in the molding of his personality. In the first few years, the infant is influenced mainly by his mother; at about the seventh year the father's influence begins to predominate. All this time, of course, other influences are also at work: the rest of the family, playmates, infant school, and the child's Faith. But in adolescence the pattern changes significantly. At this stage there is a stirring of the sense of independence. The child becomes vaguely aware of a desire for emancipation, a desire to break with the family at least for some purposes. And at this stage, the most far-reaching influences on the developing personality are precisely the groups to which he will belong, and which form, if not a substitute for, at least an auxiliary to the family. It is important in the case of the adolescent, that this tendency to emancipation should not be entirely frustrated. There should take place a gradual weaning of the child through boyhood and adolescence, so that when the time comes he will be able to stand alone before the world, a mature adult. I suggest that this weaning process is equally necessary in youth organizations. A boy can become dependent on such an organization in adolescence, as he was on the family in childhood, and may find the adjustment to adulthood extremely difficult. He should be helped sympathetically over this hurdle.

Because the "groups" to which he belongs are more immediate and more far-reaching in their effects on the developing personality in adolescence than any other single influence, one can see how important it is that the adolescent should belong to desirable and worthy groups.

Clubs and Youth Organizations are a means whereby desirable influences can be brought to bear on the boy at one of the most crucial points in his development. These influences take effect through the satisfaction of certain basic needs of the adolescent. He certainly needs a sound grounding in Christian Doctrine, and in moral training or character formation. For the first there is no adequate substitute for the laborious, sometimes heart-breaking but often consoling operation of teaching. For the latter, all the devices at our disposal in the form of cooperative and competitive group activities are efficacious.

Among the many other needs of the adolescent, I shall single out a few for special comment.

Security: This does not, of course, refer to economic security, but to emotional security. Everyone, at every age, needs this. But it is especially important in adolescence, which, psychologically speaking, is a time of the greatest insecurity. This is best achieved, I suggest, by making the boy feel that he "belongs" in the club or organization. He is not just tolerated there. He should not be made to live under a constant threat of dismissal, or of punishment or reprimand.

New Experiences: The enormously increased capacity for physical effort as well as for emotional life demands that surplus energies be drawn off somehow, and demands also that some aspects of the rich variety of the world (which is always a new world for the adolescent) be made available for him. The adolescent has an inquiring mind and all the world is before him. Give him an opportunity to explore it.

Self-esteem: He needs some grounds for thinking well of himself. This is not the same as vanity, which means thinking too well of oneself without sufficient grounds. If the adolescent has no grounds for self-esteem, we run the risk of producing weak dependent immature adults. Very often an organization can satisfy these last two needs by the same means, because it provides an opportunity for a new experience, and helps the individual boy to shine at it. If those in charge of the organization find a boy who cannot shine at any activity they provide, they should try to find something else for him, even if it is only to make him responsible for opening the window, or for calling the roll. In general, responsibility should be spread far and wide among the group. It is not necessary always to select the best boy, or the born leader when an individual has to be chosen for a special task.

Finally, one should be alive to the need for repetition of the familiar. Routine is necessary because the adolescent needs the sense of living in a world he knows, as well as the exploration of the new world opening before him. The repetition of the familiar, which may be monotonous to an adult, can contribute greatly to the security of adolescents.

4 spiritual formation of the adolescent

The more one knows of human nature the more meaningful becomes the phrase *gratia naturam non tollit sed perficit.* As a result it would appear that the more one tries to understand human nature the more one can hope to facilitate the operation of grace in forming human beings in the spiritual life. In the early days of psychology, the science suffered by reason of the fact that many of the greatest of the new psychologists were antagonistic to religion. There is a large and growing literature on the relations between psychology and religion and it seems fair to say that the issues at stake and their solutions are now fairly clear. If one assumes scientific humanism (or its older form, straight materialism) one will naturally accept Freud's *Future of an Illusion,* the main contention of which is that religion (in any form) is a neurotic manifestation of our need to defend ourselves against childish fears. If on the other hand one accepts the fact of revelation and the existence of a non-material reality, one can still profitably study the psychological process involved in both the natural and supernatural spheres, and find many parallels between them. Dr. Zilboorg did us all a great service by pinpointing the fallacy, which he called the fallacy of psychomechanistic parallelism, of identifying the two orders, natural and supernatural, on the ground that the same processes are discernible in both. It was this fallacy which underlay all attempts by psychologists to "explain away" religion simply by showing that religious behavior (including religious thinking) involved the same psychological mechanisms as other forms of behavior and thought.

Freud thought that he could show that the processes of repression, projection, rationalization and so on were common to religion and the psychoneuroses. Therefore religion itself was a psychoneurosis. Very few would now cling to this form of argument. In fact the position is quite the other way round. The same psychological mechanisms underlie the diverse functions of the mind, whether rational or irrational, normal or abnormal. We have always recognized this at the level of "ordinary" psychology. Thus the child learning to play ludo and learning arithmetic is using the same functions of perception, remembering, understanding, and may have the same emotional experience of excitement, joy, courage, or of apathy, fear, discouragement, etc. Similarly in teaching religion one uses the same psychological processes and techniques as are used in teaching arithmetic: memorizing, imaginative illustrations, intellectual comprehension, and so on. It should not be in the least surprising therefore to discover that, if we can find other deeper processes which are common to the human mind in diverse functions, these also will be helpful in teaching religion and in spiritual formation.

In adolescence, the social nature of man begins to make its demands felt for the first time. Up to this point, the family has been enough: it has provided a necessary and sufficient environment in which the individual could develop. But in adolescence this is no longer sufficient. The developing child now needs associations outside the family if he is to develop into a normally balanced and mature individual. This is not easy for him because of his shyness, awkwardness, self-consciousness. If he fails in effecting the transition from family to wider group, he may grow up to be a withdrawn, shut-in type, an *"Athanasius contra mundum"*, or a paranoid type with an ineradicable sense of grievance. If a wider society is not provided, the adolescent tends to provide it for himself, and hence the "gang" phenomenon which worries sociologists so much. The adolescent needs to belong to a group because he needs something with which he can identify himself: a set of coordinates which will serve to determine his status as a person vis-à-vis other persons, and which will provide a pattern according to which he can determine his behavior, a set of facilitating mechanisms which will minimize his bewilderment or uncertainty in new situations. He has a well-nigh insoluble task on hand: he must now achieve the desirable (and inevitable) status of being a person, independent, and incommunicable, and at the same time resist, by all the psychological devices at his disposal, the painful, conscious awareness of selfhood, independence and responsibility.

Gradually he learns how to behave, but it is still through the channels which characterized his childhood learning: introjection, identification, imitation, and not through the processes of adult learning: the acceptance of an abstract principle, and the application of it as a standard of judgment to the present concrete situation. This of course remains the ideal to aim at, but it is important to remember that even the adult only rarely behaves in this way, the adolescent almost never.

During infancy and childhood, the child has had to learn, often at considerable cost, to master his instincts and impulses. He has had to learn to master his innate aggressive impulses (e.g., not to hurt another child), to achieve a high level of control over otherwise reflex acts (to master techniques of evacuation, to acquire a rhythm of sleep), and to curb the more marked manifestations of his comparatively simple emotional life. With the onset of puberty, however, he is confronted with a much more complex task. His newly developed instinctual powers and vastly expanded capacity for emotional life both present new problems. They generate anxiety, which is nothing but fear reduced to intensity and prolonged through time. The anxiety arises because he is not yet aware of the nature and strength of these instinctual powers, nor of his ability to master them. At the same time desire and curiosity are aroused. His attitude to instinctual life becomes ambivalent: it is at once attractive and repulsive, both the attraction and repulsion being tinged with fear. The antagonism to the instincts now generated can lead to a redoubling of his efforts to master them, and this can take the form of something very closely resembling asceticism. It is not quite the mechanism of repression, for technical reasons, but it has much in common with repression. It involves for instance an ignoring of the instincts in the first part of adolescence, and this of course can be a valuable process, but it is not necessarily healthy. It can mean the deliberate avoidance of enlightenment (commoner probably with girls than with boys and of necessity involving a high level of selective inattention to the barrage of stimuli to which the adolescent is currently exposed). Essentially it is this deliberate aspect of the process which differentiates it from repression. The pseudo-asceticism which results may take the form of not caring for ordinary physical needs. The adolescent will endure extremes of cold rather than wear an overcoat; he may try to do without food or without sleep for considerable periods of time. All this can be valuable, but it requires very careful handling in order that its value may emerge. Probably for most youths in our environment it is successfully turned into something valuable, since it contributes greatly to the youth's ability to master his great difficulty, the sexual instinct. But the need for great care is evidenced by the danger that, if left to itself, this tendency may lead only to an unhealthy puritanism.

The average healthy normally-developing youth has a constitutional aversion to sexual things. True, there are always some unhealthy youths with a morbid interest in such things, but these stand out as exceptions, and in their case one will nearly always find some idiosyncratic psychogenetic factor in their psycho-sexual development to account for this. The aversion referred to here is quite compatible with a natural healthy curiosity: both are in fact aspects of the same ambivalence referred to in the previous paragraph. The psychological source of the constitutional aversion is found in the fact that the outward-regarding (or extraverted) character of the youth's psyche is more marked than his introspective tendencies, so that the instinctive movements from the deep unconscious are experienced more as frightening phenomena than as pleasurable or attractive. And this aspect of the instinctive life is reinforced by two other factors: he has already had much training in curbing aggressive influences, and, through toilet training, he has learned a great deal about the need for privacy. This constitutional aversion has much in common with the "innate" character of the virtue of modesty, on which Father Evoy, S.J., wrote a doctoral thesis for the University of Chicago.

This constitutional aversion is balanced, on the other hand, by the awakening of passionate desire. This is St. Paul's "law of my mind struggling against the law of my members", only that St. Paul is speaking about a conscious adult conflict, while we are here concerned with an unconscious adolescent one. It is this ambivalent attitude which enables us to understand the apparently inexplicable and contradictory aspects of the youth's behavior.

One should not confuse the natural asceticism and innate modesty to which I have referred with the virtues of mortification and purity. These, because virtues are habits, have to be developed by repeated acts of the will and strengthened by grace through participation in the life of grace through the sacraments, prayer, and the practices of the spiritual life generally. But clearly these natural phenomena can be of tremendous help in building a spiritual life. If, however, they are themselves mistaken for spiritual phenomena, the crash when it comes will be all the greater.

The natural healthy curiosity referred to above in connection with instinctual life is part of a wider curiosity the adolescent experiences in regard to the world in general. This wider curiosity is the source of another important aspect of the adolescent mind: its apparent intellectualism. Normally the instinctive-affective life is inversely related in intensity to the intellectual life. This means that the more the instinctive-affective life is indulged, the less (at the same time—for of course they can be consecutive) will the intellectual life flourish. But in adolescence there is an apparent reversal of this law. The reversal is only apparent, however; what appears as a fine flowering of intellectualization is really only what athletes call a "work-out". It is interesting to watch the difference between the performance of an athlete exercising himself before a high-jump, and his actual jump; or a shadow-boxing performance and the real thing. The fine intellectual performance of the adolescent discussing ideals, or politics, international affairs or religion, marriage, literature, or art, makes little or no difference to his actual behavior. Such discussions can be formal, as in a school or university debate, or informal, as in what the young American male calls a "bull session", or more informal still when a group of youths propound among themselves wild anarchic statements and draw up blueprints for the nation or the world. Clearly these exercises are largely verbal, as indeed is much of their schoolwork and study. It would be a mistake to read into them a depth or significance which, if the adolescent knew we were doing it, would only embarrass him. Anna Freud puts the matter very clearly:

"We recognize ... that we have here something quite different from intellectuality in the ordinary sense of the term. We must not suppose that an adolescent ponders on the various situations in love or on the choice of a profession in order to think out the right line of behavior, as an adult might do. . . . Adolescent intellectuality seems merely to minister to daydreams. . . . He evidently derives gratification from the mere process of thinking, speculating, or discussing. His behavior is determined by other factors and is not necessarily influenced by the results of these intellectual gymnastics." (*The Ego and the Mechanisms of Defence*, pp. 175-6.)

The situation closely resembles the pre-speech phase of babbling on the part of the infant. Like babbling, which prepares the infant for speech proper later on, these intellectual exercises of the adolescent prepare the way for real thinking later on.

It is important to note that the subjects in which the adolescent in these intellectual exercises is primarily interested are precisely those linked most closely with his anxieties. Family, friendship, love, God, religion, and power (in all its phases: leadership, politics, athletics, engines, scientific control of nature, etc.), all play a part. His difficulty is the ever-present one of "relating the instinctual side of human nature to the rest of life" (A. Freud, *loc. cit., p.* 176), of deciding to indulge or to control a sexual impulse, of choosing between liberty and restraint, between revolt and submission, obedience and disobedience. His asceticism has not solved the problem, and repression will not solve it. A temporary escape from it is achieved by "intellectualizing" it. This enables him to turn to his conflict in thought, instead of running away from it or yielding in actual behavior to the pressure of instinct. Hence "the abstract intellectual discussions and speculations in which young people delight are not genuine attempts at solving the tasks set by reality". But they can be most valuable nevertheless. They serve to turn instinctual processes into conceptual thinking, and so render them accessible to consciousness. This is the very first requisite in making them amenable to control, and eventually bringing them under the control of the will. The apparent asceticism, the constitutional aversion, the "innate modesty", and all the other defense mechanisms to which one might refer derive from the non-rational, or better pre-rational, instinctual, unconscious part of us. They are not fully "human acts". But when intellect, through conceptual thinking, begins to grapple with them, and will can choose appropriate lines of action, the moral quality of the resultant behavior changes. It would clearly be a mistake to build too much on their instinctual, pre-rational, natural character.

Such then in brief is the phenomenon we are dealing with: an individual human being, who must not be thought of as a miniature adult but only as a potential one, with problems and processes specific to his own age-group. We must now consider his spiritual formation.

It is noteworthy, at the outset, that there have been very few indeed canonized from this age-group. St. Dominic

Savio comes to mind, and Maria Goretti, Stanislaus Kostka, and perhaps one or two more—but a very great number has been canonized from the next age-group: the young adults. The reason for this is not difficult to find. Apart from martyrdom, sanctity is achieved through heroic virtue, and the exercise of the virtues is through human acts, whereas, as we have seen, much of the behavior of the adolescent, even when it is good and savors of merit, is still largely instinctive rather than voluntary. In training adolescents, moreover, it is important to remember that young people generally will tend to behave in the ways in which we expect them to behave, rather than in the ways in which we tell them to behave. They do this through two mechanisms: on the one hand through empathy—they feel our lack of confidence in them; and on the other, through identification: they observe the contradictions in our own lives between performance and precept, and identify with us at our level of achievement rather than our level of aspiration. It is obvious, therefore, that if we are to succeed in training adolescents, we must reorientate our own thinking first.

Furthermore, it is obvious that knowledge is not virtue. We can give, and young people can receive, almost passively, a great deal of knowledge. But the acquisition of virtue must come from within, and actively—from autodetermined action at the level of human acts. This means consciously chosen, willed acts, with knowledge of the substance and end and all the relevant ethical determinants. Do we ever in fact provide opportunities for this kind of act? True, opportunities will arise for the adolescent. But do we try to provide them, in the way in which we provide training for a football team, or illustrations for history or geography? I do not mean, do we tell them moral tales or goody-goody stories? It would not be difficult to think up ethical or moral problems, analogous to the *casus* of moral theology, but of course much simpler and more direct, more immediately relevant to the adolescent's world. This could be done in the form of questions at the end of a class on the commandments, for instance: "What would you do if you found a purse in the street?", "If you found at the end of the day that you had not worked hard enough to earn your salary?", "If you knew that your team was fielding a disqualified man?", "If you broke a window?", etc., etc., naturally geared in difficulty to the different age-groups.

This kind of training could be supplemented by more concrete methods. These of course will not involve situations where a breach would involve sin, but where nevertheless a conscious choice at the level of human actions has to be made. In homework, or study preparation, for example, an occasional piece of work could be given for which the solution is available in some textbook at the disposal of the students. The students might be told: "You may take this from your books if you wish, but if you do, mark your exercise with an 'X'. . . ." This confronts the youth with a choice which is very real and which is very tempting in one direction. It is only on rare occasions that the adolescent is presented with situations where the raw act of the will is fully conscious. Discipline is necessary for the adolescent, as is routine. But the experienced teacher can think up a thousand ways in which open choices are presented, without endangering good order and discipline.

In teaching religion to adolescents, and in preaching to them, it is important to avoid the importation of emotional elements. By this I do not imply that emotion is bad or undesirable. I mean only that the emotions we may import will be the wrong ones. We will only succeed in embarrassing the young people, thus producing negativism or worse. Heartiness and humor (unless it is extremely cleverly done) will be just as embarrassing as sentiment or mawkishness. Many of the mysteries of religion are emotional enough in their own right: Bethlehem, Calvary, mortal sin, Hell, etc. But the adolescent strives to conceal his emotions because he is afraid of them. He will avoid the more tender emotions with particular care because he cannot be sure of his own responses, as witness his avoidance of affection for mother or sister in public. With regard to sin and Hell, he is already suffering conflicts in their regard. It would be a pity to aggravate these conflicts for that will not resolve them. The desirable approach is a cool, dead-panning attitude in which the teacher's position is plainly and unequivocally one of "What I am saying to you is a set of true propositions", and not one of "What I am saying to you is an exhortation, or moral uplift". There are two points to be stressed here. One is the difficulty of identifying a genuine act of faith in an adolescent. The other is the immediacy of his awareness of temporal punishment, both through emotional guilt and through his experience of disciplinary measures. The first point means something like this: the adolescent does of course make acts of faith since he has the infused theological virtues through Baptism and Confirmation. But we, looking on from the outside, can be easily misled. To the adolescent, at any rate in early adolescence, there is no more mystery about the spiritual world than there is about outer space, no more mystery about Transubstantiation than there is about the conversion of mass into energy in the atom bomb. This of course is a good thing, and I do not wish to suggest that we should put difficulties into his mind. What I mean is something quite different and much more general. The intellect reaches its peak point of development in adolescence and the adolescent has a clearer eye than we have for spiritual things. Like the disciples on the road to Emmaus, his eyes can be opened (Luke xxiv, 31). Adolescents have the grace of God and the indwelling of the Holy Ghost to help them; they have the gifts of wisdom, understanding, and knowledge. We can therefore give them a great deal more than we usually do. The more we give, the more they can take. We are sometimes tempted to confuse what the adolescent ought to be able to repeat or reproduce with what he ought to know. This is an elementary pedagogic mistake. The adolescent can take something very close to the content of a lecture on dogmatic theology. He should not, therefore, be limited to a few abbreviated shorthand notes. If he is given the full richness of the Church's teaching on some mystery, for example Transubstantiation, he will penetrate very far indeed into it. It will then be possible to insist on the memorizing and reproducing process in a meaningful way. But sometimes at least, all he is given is what he is expected to reproduce. It is at this level that the danger may arise about the act of faith. Christian Doctrine should be taught to adolescents at an adult level. We have already accepted this in regard to algebra, geometry, the calculus, literature, etc., and we take it for granted. For a generation or more, we have been teaching material to youths at school which up to recently was difficult for adults. We have not yet decided, in teaching religion, to be as wise as the children of this world.

There is an incidental consideration to be made here. Some teachers tend to import into their teaching of religion two elements of anxiety which have no place there. First, because of the importance of the subject they are themselves anxious about it, and may communicate this anxiety to their pupils. The second anxiety is the generation in some schools of an examination greater even than that which arises with regard to secular subjects. Examinations are, of course, necessary. But the teaching of religious knowledge should be a model subject in the school, and not a frantic fear-laden cram three weeks before the examination. How many schools put their very best teachers in charge of this subject?

In the spiritual formation of the adolescent, the main dangers and difficulties should now be fairly obvious.

First, there is the danger of confusing a purely naturalistic approach with a supernatural one. The adolescent has anxieties and difficulties of his own. He may discover, or we may communicate to him, that he can find relief for his anxieties in religious practices. He may tend to use religion for this purpose, to the possible detriment of religion itself in the long run, for it will not necessarily relieve anxiety, and it is not its formal function to do so. He may discover that it does not do so in his case (as apparently James Joyce did) and then turn away from it altogether, at least for a time. The maturation process can easily be delayed through this naturalistic use of religion.

Secondly, there is the danger of mere conformity. This is familiar to most teachers, and most school authorities take precautions against it. This danger arises because of the adolescent's need, referred to above, for group-structure, group-organization, and identification. He will be enormously helped in this by group-organizations such as sodalities. But membership of these organizations should not be confused with meritorious human acts. There may be only a minimum of human volition and free choice involved. Such organizations are a means to an end: the end being the inducing of free human choices on the adolescent's part. If they do not do this, they will have failed. The enormous number of young people who cease (temporarily) to practice their religion after leaving school would seem to indicate that the organizational method has not succeeded in making their religion for them a matter of personal choice. (Many of them make a clear choice again later on, usually on the occasion of marriage, so that it would be a mistake to think that the method has failed entirely.)

Thirdly, the apparent intellectualism of the adolescent is obviously important in the context of spiritual formation. It means that one will naturally expect to find the adolescent expressing an interest in spiritual things, a readiness to read spiritual books, to discuss spiritual topics, etc. But it would be a mistake to take this too readily as a sign of spirituality. It may mean no more than a similar interest in space fiction or romantic literature. And even if it is more than this and represents a genuine interest in spiritual things, it may have little or no influence on behavior. It may represent a transient interest rather than an abiding need. I would not like to suggest that the adolescent should be discouraged from spiritual reading, but it might be a good thing to discourage him from reading spiritual books written for adolescents. These are usually well-intentioned, but sometimes rather frothy, especially in their presentation of adolescent saints. It should be remembered that the intellect, as was said above, reaches its peak point of development in adolescence. Playing down to the adolescent can only result in harm. He will turn away in disgust from what he will regard as "sissy" writing. People who write books on religion and spirituality for adolescents should read the kind of things provided for adolescents in astronomy, archaeology, space travel, science fiction. Only the best lives of the saints and spiritual books should be given to the interested adolescent. The emphasis for the moment should in general be on inculcating the natural virtues: manliness, honesty, reliability, fair-dealing, etc. In this way a solid basis will be laid down for spiritual development. If this is not done, much effort will be wasted on ephemeral and accidental matters.

Prayer is one of the most difficult topics to discuss accurately in reference to the adolescent. The obvious danger is that we may teach the adolescent to use prayer as a rationalization rather than as a spiritual exercise. The difficulty is one of drawing the line, and I do not wish to exaggerate. We do not let the adolescent think that he is going to pass his examinations merely by doing novenas. And most of his prayer is probably sanctifying and efficacious. But his anxieties are not automatically relieved or cured by prayer, nor is he necessarily helped into adulthood by the kind of prayer he most often uses: prayer of petition. The adult seeking peace of mind or peace of soul generally knows what he is seeking. His search is a rational one, and for many it will also be supernaturalized. He seeks forgiveness for conscious wrong-doing, or perhaps greater certainty about God's mercy. His anxiety may very well be the *timor Domini* which is the beginning of wisdom. If his anxiety has a natural source in his own emotional life, this will not surprise him. He can cope with it, and in praying for peace of mind he will not apply the test of freedom from a natural emotional upset as a criterion of the degree of efficacy, in prayer. But it is otherwise with the adolescent.

In general, the normal adult will not think that the value of his prayer is proportioned to the physical intensity he can put into the act of "saying a prayer", nor is he still subject to the magic words (a childhood phenomenon) to the same extent as the adolescent. "Open Sesame" as an efficient cause capable of opening a locked door presents no difficulty to a child. This type of word-magic survives in the meaningless expletives (or even meaningful obscenities and curses, and conventional phrases such as "cheers", "good luck") of the adult, which serve as efficient means of relieving one's feelings. The average adult does not perhaps realize that the latter are word-magic similar to "Open Sesame". The adolescent comes somewhere between the overtly magical use of language by the child, and the automatic ritualistic quasi-magical use of the adult. He does not really believe in "Open Sesame" but he does not reject the possible efficacy of a wish to bring about a desirable state of affairs. He does not really believe that calling somebody a nasty name will turn the person into the corresponding thing. But he has his own taboo words (usually common to a group, gang, or school), and he usually accepts some form of sympathetic magic. He must be led to discriminate between prayer and word-magic.

It should be clear, therefore, that one must be extremely careful about adolescent prayer. If an adult is in danger of using prayer as a wish-fulfillment, the danger is even greater for the adolescent, since he is in any case prone to indulge grandiose fantasies in daydreaming. Romanticizing the priest-hood or the missions or the Life of Our Lord can serve to feed the imagination rather than to deepen the spiritual life. Prayer can be a successful outlet for the adolescent's emotional drives, and for the pseudo-intellectualization described earlier in this essay. Sublimation is one of the few defense mechanisms which can serve healthy purposes, but the wise director will not encourage it. Finally, one must ensure that prayer does not partake of a compulsive-obsessional character. Should it do so, to that extent it ceases to be profitable or a genuine act of worship. This can easily arise if too much stress is laid on repetitive vocal prayer, and especially true of youths in the late teens who are already in process of formation as ecclesiastical students. The dangers I have been underlining are on the whole the dangers of a minority, at any rate in acute forms. I do not wish to suggest that all, or even a great number, fall into them. The vulnerable group is in any case always a minority group, and it is from the minority group that problems arise.

Because of the keenness of his intellect the adolescent will almost inevitably encounter doubts and difficulties about religious matters. It is only too easy to teach him to repress these doubts and to rationalize his difficulties. This is a mistake. It should be explained to him that a doubt in his mind is really a question: a seeking of further enlightenment, not a rejection of faith. It is an occasion for the deliberate exercise of an act of faith. A difficulty likewise should serve as an occasion for the deeper penetration of the mystery, and adolescents should be led to understand that the great theologians advanced our knowledge of God and the spiritual world by a combination of prayer and the facing of difficulties. This does not mean that every alleged difficulty and doubt should be treated equally seriously. Adolescents delight in playing the game of trying to stump the teacher. A little experience will enable the teacher or spiritual director to discriminate between the genuine question and the game. Moreover, most of the adolescent's difficulties about religion are not theological difficulties, but moral or mental health problems.

In this chapter I have not been concerned about expounding the well-proven principles of the spiritual life: the necessity of regular participation in spiritual exercises, of mortification, of mental prayer, of the examination of conscience, and the exercise of the virtues. My concern has been to try, rather, to show something of the nature of the adolescent to whom we must expound these principles. There is every reason to hope that the deepening insights into the adolescent mind now available may be of great help in teaching religion and in the spiritual formation of young people. *Timentibus Deum, omnia cooperantur in bonum.*

5 chemistry and personality

The number of distinguished scientists in our day who, having pursued their scientific work to the limit of their very great competence, have found themselves impelled to enter the speculative field of philosophy is startling. One thinks of Einstein's *The World As I See It*, of Eddington's *Philosophy of Physical Science*, Max Born on *Physics and Metaphysics*, Schroedinger on the philosophical problem of the existence of elementary particles, and more to our purpose, Sherrington's *Man on His Nature*, or Eccles' *The Neurophysiological Basis of Mind*. The number of contemporary philosophers, on the other hand, who have entered the domain of the sciences, is small. Broad tried to master physics for his *Mind and Its Place in Nature*. Russell was a good mathematician and tried also to integrate philosophy and physics, but without much success. Most logicians try to understand the methodology of the sciences, but it remains true that few philosophers achieve even a moderate competence in scientific matters.

In order to pinpoint the area with which I shall be concerned, I shall put before you two quotations, one from a psychologist and the other from a physiologist. The psychologist is Gardner Murphy. "Quite apart from all theories as to the relation of mind and body, the subject matter of psychology and the subject matter of physiology are already merging, and seem likely before long to become simply one subject matter—the quantitative laws of the organism. It is, perhaps, not entirely fanciful to suggest that as our knowledge and our language become more precise, the answer to the question: How much does it hurt? may be 42 xy3Cos A."

While I would not like to suggest that this is the considered and mature view of Gardner Murphy, it is nevertheless a point of view which is gaining ground, and seems to raise problems of far-reaching consequence. Contrast this view with that of Sherrington. Expounding his view of mind as immaterial, he goes on: "(I prefer to think that) the theoretically impossible happens: mind acts on matter and matter on mind. My mind bends my arm, and disturbs the sun just as, through my retina and brain, the sun acts on my mind. We have to accept the correlation (between physical and mental events) and to view it as interaction." (*Man on His Nature*, 1951.) Adrian is a little more cautious, calling it concomitance, rather than interaction. "The physiologist," he says, "cannot look at the problem (of the relation between a particular pattern of nerve-impulses and an idea, or brain and mind) except as a natural scientist, and at present that seems almost certain to lead him into trouble." (*Contribution to The Physical Basis of Mind*, ed. Laslett, 1950.)

It is interesting to note that the philosophers, led by Gilbert Ryle of Oxford, have been very busy recently trying to exorcise the ghost of Cartesian dualism from the machine of the contemporary physiologist and biochemist, while the physiologists, neurophysiologists, and biochemists have been trying harder than ever to find some way of accomodating the ghost in the so much more complicated machine than Descartes ever thought of. It was Ryle's contention that all talk about a mind was misleading and due to a simple mistake which he called the Category Mistake. We were led to think of MIND, because we kept asking the wrong question, as though a person who had seen all the individual colleges of Oxford were then to go on and ask: Now please show me the University. When, in other words, we had seen all the activities which we call mental, we were tempted to say: Now please show me the mind. It is Ryle's contention that mind simply is these activities, just as the University simply is the Colleges, not something set up side by side with, or anterior to, them. Yet Ryle would probably say he was neither a Behaviorist nor a Materialist. However, the really amusing aspect of the situation in contemporary thought arises from the fact that those who know most about the body and its activities are precisely those most inclined to attempt the Herculean task of finding a place for the ghost in it.

I shall not attempt to summarise even a fraction of the literature now available on the organism and its physico-chemical functions. But I shall have to indicate briefly something of the nature of the problem of the relation of chemistry and personality as it appears from the empirical evidence. Always it is the same problem, with a new vocabulary and a more detailed statement, and always the same solutions are offered. My contention is that some of those who appear to be speaking on the side of the angels, raise more difficulties than they appear to solve.

From the biochemist, we learn more and more about the biochemistry of the cell, and since the living body is composed of cells, logically the biochemistry of the cell may be presumed to throw a great deal of light eventually even on the nature of life itself. The functioning of the endocrine glands has for a long time now been recognized as a major determining factor in the production of the personality, as we observe it at any point in its maturation. And we know that the particular pattern of endocrine functioning, apart from environmental influences which may modify it in known ways, is determined by genetic inheritance. A further step can now be taken in the logic of this development. The importance of the group of macro-molecular substances called nucleic acids is recognized in this context, first because these can now be partially synthetized, and second, because apparently an intelligible picture can be given of their function in heredity. It is suggested that the very genic substance itself, borne by the chromosomes, may be deoxyribonucleic acid (Avery, 1944). Let me quote Sir Alexander Todd: "The past five years have seen an astonishing revolution in the field (of the nucleic acids) and one which has put our knowledge of nucleic acid structure on a firm foundation and brought it to a point where it stands comparison with our knowledge of the proteins." Earlier, Sir Alexander had said: "They (the nucleic acids) occur at times free, but more often in association with proteins, as the so-called nucleo-proteins. These, probably the most complex of all substances of biological origin, include enzymes and viruses. . . ." The virus raises a further problem. It has been contended that the viruses represent the link between the organic and the inorganic (though this, apparently, is not the current view). So that what we have thought of as a real substantial essential difference—the difference between life and non-life—becomes one merely of degree of complexity of structure. This had often been contended by philosophers of course, notably by Leibniz (1648-1716). It is a point of view which finds curious confirmation in unexpected places. It is manifest that the organism is material, whatever else might be said about it. Equally manifest therefore, should be the proposition that whatever is true of matter will be true of organism. This will mean in effect that the organism will be analysable in the long run into atoms and their elementary particles. Sherrington is obviously puzzled by this, and he states it so felicitously that I shall quote him. He is referring to a well-known passage in Eddington, where he speaks of his table and of his elbow resting on it. "True," says Sherrington, "there is between the elbow and the table the difference that the one is living and the other is dead. Chemistry and physics say nothing of this. Or rather they say a great deal about it, but do not in saying it make use of either of these words. If we tell them that the table was at one time living wood and is now dead wood, that the wood was at one time part of a living tree, they do not recognize the word as conveying any radical distinction between the two. . . . Chemistry says that neither in the one case nor in the other does it find any thing or any behavior which is not chemical."

It is now, I take it, practically impossible to say where physics ends and chemistry begins—there is no real distinction between them. The elementary particles of the physicist are explanatory of a whole range of phenomena, and serve as a unifying set of concepts to bring together into focus the different sciences which deal with man. (I know that Schroedinger has seen fit to call in question the very existence of these elementary particles in a series of papers which, because of their philosophical difficulty, have not received the attention they deserve, and I know that this point of view of his has been labeled as "reactionary" by Max Born. However, that is not my problem, and moreover, even if the elementary particles are superseded by some alternative set of concepts, these latter will still be concepts of matter or material process, and the fundamental problem will remain unaltered).   The fundamental problem to which I refer can be stated like this: If the study of the organism is in the long run chemistry, and if chemistry in the long run is physics, then the organism and all its movements must be subject to the laws of physics. (I am not going to get involved in the problem of free-will versus determinism. This latter problem is only a small consequential difficulty, rather than the real focus of the problem.) There is no reason to suppose, from an examination of physics qua physics, that the human body will be, alone among material things, exempt from physical law. There has occasionally been an appeal to the Uncertainty Principle as a way out of this difficulty, but the appeal is vain, first because the very principle itself is a law of the behavior of matter, and second, because if the law applies to the organism at all, as it surely must, it does so precisely because it, the organism, is material. Hinshelwood, among others, has been tempted to see a way out in the very abstractness of physical knowledge itself. I quote: "It may reasonably be said that a purely materialist attitude seems rather more hopeless than ever in view of the abstractness of the fundamental laws which chemistry and physics have discovered." This seems to put Hinshelwood on the side of the angels, but for illusory reasons. In fact the statement is a complete *nonsequitur*. The laws which chemistry and physics have discovered are laws about the structure and function of matter, and are presumably in large measure valid. But how do they make a materialist attitude, "more hopeless than ever"? The laws of modern symbolic logic are even more abstract still, as also are the laws of pure mathematics, but in themselves they neither confirm nor serve to reject the materialist hypothesis. If Hinshelwood had said:

"The fact that we can come to know such laws, or even to know the most elementary fact of our experience, effectively negatives the materialist hypothesis," we might be tempted to agree, but then we would no longer be speaking as physicists or chemists, but as professional philosophers occupied with epistemology. But that is not my problem at the moment.

Let me put the matter in the strongest possible terms. Accepting that reality is knowable, and that therefore the organism is knowable and knowable without limit, and postulating adequate, or even infinite time if necessary, there is nothing in theory or in logic to set a limit to the amount and degree of knowledge which will be acquired about the physics and chemistry of the organism. This sort of consideration, varying in detail from age to age, has been part of the haunting dream of Western Man from Pygmalion to Frankenstein. I do not see that in this respect modern physics or chemistry has raised any new philosophical problem. If one could assemble all the particles of the organism in test-tubes or in the laboratory, and if one could achieve the correct structure and the requisite functional unity and interdependence, one would have the living body. Or would one? The difficulty is not in the series of hypotheses, but in the naive translating of the "if we would" into "we can", plus a tacit ignoring altogether of the third condition. Raising this as a philosophical problem is what I call sometimes "basing hypotheses on the phenomena revealed by hopes."

However, assuming that physiology, through chemistry, and chemistry through physics, have achieved their final statements about the organism, there are two sets of phenomena to be considered. "All that remains in the chemist's substratum of things seem to be geometry, motion and number. This does not mean that chemistry teaches any disregard for these qualities which are of such importance to human beings. It simply refers them to the world of mind." (Hinshelwood.) It is this world of mind I would now turn to.

There is a naive view of the relation of the world of mind to the physical world we have been considering, which goes something like this: There is a physical world with its own laws, and having certain sense-qualities out there, independent of my thinking and of yours. The laws of this world are discovered with great difficulty, but the sense-qualities are given immediately in sense-experience. "Things" affect the body, and the changes in the body affect the mind, with the result that the mind comes to know the things. Interaction between body and mind is assumed, and it is assumed to be a two-way street. This is what Sherrington assumes to be "theoretically impossible", and which he nevertheless asserts happens. The scientific point of view considerably alters the picture. First, we are confronted with the apparent non-objectivity of the sense-energy of nerves' theory associated with Muller and Helmolz, and its more recent developments in terms of electronics, by Adrian and Eccles and others. A set of impulses is discharged by a receptor organ, which after various synaptic relays, evokes a specific spatio-temporal pattern of impulses in the neuronal network of the cerebral cortex. The transmission from receptor organ to cerebral cortex is by a coded pattern that is quite unlike the original stimulus, and the pattern in the cortex is again different from this. Usually at this point the physiologist adds some phrase, which however it may be formulated, amounts to saying: "At this point the sensation passes over into consciousness."

I do not know any physiologist, biochemist, or chemist,

who has denied this,* but neither do I know any who has given an intelligible account of consciousness or its relation to the body. True, Sherrington asserts without comment or evidence, "that the brain is the bodily organ of the mind we have to accept as an established fact," and I expect that most physiologists would agree, but in actual fact the evidence does no more than indicate that mental process is somehow more closely related to the brain than, say, to the rest of the CNS, or the rest of the organism. Eccles assumes that "liaison (between brain and mind) occurs only in special states of the matter-energy system of the cerebral cortex" (p. 267), and that these are certain "dynamic patterns of neuronal activity that occur in the cerebral cortex curing conscious states," but this seems to be a vicious circle, as well as a complete ignoring of the phenomena of mind in unconscious states. But Eccles' general theory will need some further comment later, so we can let this go for the moment.

Adrian is alive to the difficulties that arise out of statements of this kind (cf. "Arguments which jump from the physical to the mental plane are continually landing us into difficulties"). But in spite of his own warning, he lapses at times into precisely the same mode of thought: "The part of our picture of the brain which may always be missing ... is the part which deals with the mind, that part which ought to explain how a particular pattern of nerve impulses can produce an idea; or the other way round, how a thought can decide which nerve cells are to come into action." Russell

---

* But see Lashley: Hixon Symposium, 1951. "Our common meeting ground is the faith to which we all subscribe. I believe that the phenomena of behavior and mind are ultimately describable in the concepts of the mathematical and physical sciences." This seems to be a clear statement of a purely materialistic point of view, but few would go the whole way with it, I think.

Brain speaks of "changes in the physiology of the brain", "producing" proportionate changes in consciousness. Penfield is, perhaps, the clearest of all: "Something else," he says, "finds its dwelling place between the sensory complex and the motor mechanism . . . there is a switchboard operator as well as a switchboard."

It is time now to look at a different sort of problem—the problems that arise from the phenomena revealed in psychology and allied branches of study. I have already mentioned the endocrine glands and their influence on personality. The effects of narcosis, pentothal, ECT, insulin coma, etc. on the mental process have received wide publicity, so I shall not dwell on them. "Almost every aspect of cerebral activity is open to chemical modification," says McIlwain, (*Biochemistry and the Central Nervous System,* 1955). It has been suggested that mescaline can produce personality changes of the same order as those observed as a result of brain-washing techniques in Eastern European trials, and the disorders of perception resulting from it are familiar to readers in Huxley. I shall give a recent and striking example of the relation of chemistry to personality, which is coming into some prominence in psychiatry. Lycergic acid diethylamide (produced synthetically from lycergic acid, the polycyclic substance common to the ergot alkaloids) taken intravenously in very small doses, causes usually a prompt change in blood adrenaline without much change in blood glucose. There are other effects too, such as an accumulation of Hexose monophosphate, but these are not our concern. The adrenaline drops in 5 to 10 minutes, followed by a rise which on the average becomes maximal at 60 minutes. Now consider the mental phenomena: hallucinations occur, together with marked changes of mood, a condition resembling schizophrenia. Panic, anxiety and terror accompany the rise in adrenaline. The condition of mentally ill subjects is temporarily aggravated, schizophrenics apparently showing increased withdrawal and tension or precipitation of catatonia. (I am indebted for the above to psychiatric friends and to McIlwain, *loc. cit.*)

The brain is the richest or one of the richest mammalian tissues in serotonin (like lycergic acid, one of the beta-phenylethylamine derivatives), which is an antagonist of lycergic acid. Is the artificially induced schizophrenia-like ophrenia, therefore, due simply to the presence or absence in cortical tissue of lycergic acid or serotonin? Clearly it is too early to say, and one must be on guard against the fallacy of plurality of causes. One hopes that it might be so, but even should it turn out to be so, is any new problem raised about the relation of mind to matter? or any new light thrown on the problem? I think not. For I can see no way, relevant to the problem of mind-matter, in which such knowledge differs logically or philosophically from the ordinary citizen's knowledge of the effects of alcohol.

Most striking in some respects, and perhaps more helpful in our understanding of mind, is the drug Chlorpromazine. Chlorpromazine was synthetized as a result of a systematic search for a chemical compound of the phenothiazine group with special effects of the nervous system. This drug counteracts and reverses the effects of adrenaline. Among its somatic effects one notes: dryness of the mouth, constipation, polyuria, drowsiness, a drop in the oxygen-consumption of the braincells, etc. From the psychological point of view its importance lies in the fact that while the patient's emotional states are reduced in intensity, and motor activity and wakefulness are decreased, this is done apparently without significantly interfering with higher psychic functions. It is tempting to regard this as evidence at last from the empirical-experimental plane for the contention that thought as such is independent of matter. It would be impressive to couple this finding with the failure of the electroencephalograph to reveal any change correlated with high-level thought process corresponding to the consistent changes related to flicker or emotion, and conclude that here at last is proof of the existence of mind or soul—indeed it is surprising that the physiologists referred to above have not already done so in their eagerness to rehabilitate the ghost in the machine. But it would be fallacious to do so, for the very good reason that physical detectors will only detect physical things, and their non-detection of the mind or soul or ghost is certainly no proof of its existence.

It is very often assumed (e.g., by Sherrington) that the self, or ego, is given in immediate experience, and that "Mental experiences" in the words of Russell Brain, "are the events in the universe of which we have the most direct knowledge." This would be attractive if it were true. But I question it even on the plane of pure phenomenology, or the analysis of experience. What is given in immediate experience is always either a mental content or process and the consciousness of self or ego is a rather high-level emergent end-result. Clearly babies have not got it, nor mental defectives, nor animals. And even the mental contents and processes from which it is inferred are not given as mental. What is experienced is something trans-subjective. The becoming aware of the sphere of the mental is a reflective act; it is a consequence of the awareness of self or ego.

This notion of the self or ego leads me to the next consideration. So far we have been concerned with the apparent movement from matter to mind. But there is an equally impressive body of evidence apparently showing the effects of mind on matter. I am not thinking of Sherrington's naive "my mind bends my arm." He says: "Physics tell me that unless my mind is energy it cannot disturb the sun. My mind then does not bend my arm. If it does, the theoretically impossible happens. Let me prefer to think that the theoretically impossible does happen. Despite the theoretical I take it my mind does bend my arm, and that it disturbs the sun." It is rather difficult for a philosopher to see how a scientist can accept the theoretically impossible, the obvious self-contradiction. It seems clear that Sherrington is prepared to go to great lengths to stay on the side of the angels, and it strikes me that many scientists have to face the same dilemma, and, perhaps, take the same easy way out. The acceptance of a self-contradiction has happened before. I take it that at least some nineteenth century scientists must have felt the contradictions inherent in the notion of the ether. John Stuart Mill explicitly and consciously accepted the contradiction inherent in the theory which he had taken from Hume, that mind is nothing but a series of conscious states, the earlier phases of the series being over and done with and past history before the present state comes into being and yet that this series was capable of becoming conscious of itself as a series. Again, the practicing analyst is very often constrained to accept contradictions or modify his theories. There is no doubt that in our naive thinking we are all inclined to accept the apparent contradiction that mind, if it is what we think it is, is dimensionless, non-extended, non-material, and therefore incapable of disposing of physical energy; and to accept that the laws of conservation of matter, of energy, of force, are universally valid, even with the necessary provisos imposed by quantum physics; and at the same time, to accept that mind acts on matter and matter on mind. What it comes to is that Sherrington is either abandoning the validity of these laws in physicism or else inventing a new physics. Pirenne has shown that Eccles is in much the same position. But I shall come to Eccles in due course. What it comes to is this: either there must be something wrong with Sherrington's physics or with his philosophy. Now it seems much more likely that his physics will be right and his philosophy absurd, because he is a trained scientist, but not a trained philosopher. The same criticism could be applied to many others.

The time is passed when analytic theory could be rejected out of hand with a self-righteous polemic against pan-sexuality, or on the other hand, forced on the critical student by the device of suggesting that if he rejected it, it was because of his own complexes and unconsciously-motivated resistances. Analytic theory is a body of doctrine concerning the nature and dynamics of certain kinds of mental content, some of the processes, conscious and unconscious, which go on in every mind, and the genesis of certain conditions (which may be either psychical or physical or both) which are symptomatic of the unhealthy functioning of these processes. When the symptoms are predominantly physical, one speaks variously either of conversion symptoms, conversion hysteria, or psychosomatic medicine. The concepts here are again an extension of our naive thinking. It seems obvious that when we feel shy we blush—the emotion "causes" the physical symptom. When we feel afraid, the pulse races, the blood sugar drops, the respiration rate increases, certain blood vessels contract, and there occur many chemical changes while the endocrine glands are mobilizing their forces. And we say the emotion "caused" all these. This theory depends, notice, on the assumption that an emotion is a mental phenomenon, and that such a mental phenomenon is capable of causing changes in the physical universe. This theory is applied to the symptoms mentioned above. The theory is that the physical symptom is either a translation of a repressed psychical item into a physical one, or is the physical effect of a psychical cause. It is not necessary to go into detail, as I take it that popular journalism has acquainted us all sufficiently with this sort of phenomenon. The idea is that "prolonged anxiety produces a duodenal ulcer," that "a repressed emotion can produce a localized anaesthesia or a localized paralysis without any physical lesion or cause." It is the opposite in a way of our theory earlier on, that a purely physical phenomenon such as a lycergic acid-serotonin imbalance can produce a mental illness.

In the presence of such theories, the intelligent physician or surgeon must pause. Either he accepts the possibility which his physics and chemistry and his knowledge of physiology and biochemistry tell him is impossible, i.e. the possibility that a purely mental phenomenon can produce a physiological lesion, or he accepts two concomitant, contemporaneous series of events which run parallel to each other, but are otherwise unrelated, or he rejects the purely mental altogether. He may feel reluctantly compelled to accept a sort of unacknowledged materialism, or like Watson, Lashley, and others, uncompromising materialism, or with Sherrington to commit himself expressly to the acceptance of an irrational self-contradiction. Probably, many, if not most, reach the compromise of the two unrelated series of events. This was put forward seriously as a philosophical position by Leibniz, but can easily be shown to involve absurd consequences, including pan-psychism and the most rigid form of determinism.

The problem around which I have centered this essay is one of the oldest, most difficult, and most important that the human mind can face. And it seems to me fairly obvious that there is no ground for supposing that the most difficult and important problems will have easy answers. You will, perhaps, have noted that I tried to pose the problem in its contemporary form. But I could have posed it in terms of Democritus, Plato and Aristotle in Greek times, or in terms of St. Thomas, Scotus, and the Averroists in Medieval times, or in terms of Descartes, Leibniz, and Hume in the modern era. The problem as I have put it to you, arising out of the contemporary evidence, is due directly to Descartes and his formulation of it. When Penfield faces the issue of the relation of mind and matter in connection with sensation, he concludes: "Something else" finds its dwelling place between the sensory complex and the motor mechanism. . . . "There is a switchboard operator as well as a switchboard." Now this switchboard operator of Penfield haunts the thinking of nearly all those who have considered this problem. He is the "observer" who receives sensations; he is the "ego" of the analyst who is the plaything of the impulses of the organism or "id"; he is the little man in the brain, the homunculus, who is "me" conceived as operating the puppet of the body; he is "consciousness" who intervenes between the stimulus and response mechanism; he is Descartes' "soul" which is a geometrical point, located in the pineal gland, and interacts with the body through the animal spirits. Very often he is thought of as me or you, imprisoned for a time in the prison-house of the flesh, awaiting his release, so that he can return to his proper abode whence he came in the first instance.

Descartes was a very great physiologist, as well as a very great mathematician. And he was also a very logical thinker. Were there space, it would be helpful to expound his philosophy, and explain just how and why he came to hold the position he did. The reader would then understand why he, together with nearly all those I have named so far, are at heart good Cartesians. But rather inconsistent ones, I suggest. Let me quote a few sentences from Descartes. "The body," he asserts, "is a machine made by the hands of God." (*Discourse* 5). A change in a bodily organ "can be nothing else but the motion of the particles of the sensory organs and the change of figure and position due to that motion." (*Reply to obj.* 6.) The motion set up in the nerves passes to "the extremities of those nerves which are collected in the brain by the nerves affect the soul or mind" (*Prin.* 2). The particular sensation that arises depends on the nerve stimulated and on the movements made in each nerve. "We do not discover that anything other than these motions ever passes from the organs of the external senses to the brain." Translate the terms into contemporary neurological formulations and reduce these in turn to their physico-chemical elements and you have the position which would, I think, be defended by any contemporary writer on the subject. The position is attractive (as Pirenne points out) because it seems to save the existence of mind, while regarding the body as a purely material-mechanical system. Descartes, being logical, faced the obvious conclusion that I must either postulate a soul for animals other than man which would also have to be a spirit, or else come down explicitly on the side of asserting that animals are mere automata, incapable of anything save purely mechanical physico-chemical processes. They would have to be incapable not only of knowledge and consciousness, but also of pain and sorrow and joy and suffering, or else other material compositions would have to be credited with these.

Eccles is the most recent scientist to grapple with the problem. In the last chapter of his *Neurophysiological Basis of Mind* (The Waynflete Lectures of 1952), he tackles the problem valiantly. He is very anxious to defend not only mind, but also free will and consciousness. He postulates that for "will" to be operative, large populations of cortical neurones are subjected to an intensive synaptic bombardment, and are stimulated therefore to discharge impulses which bombard other neurones. He argues convincingly that the pattern of discharge of hundreds of thousands of neurones could be modified as a result of an "influence" that initially caused the discharge of merely one neurone, and an integration of the activity of a whole network of hundreds of thousands of neurones could take place in a few milliseconds. Analogous considerations are put forward for the more general concept of the relation of mind to the cortex. The idea is that the brain is equipped with detectors for minute fields of influence spread over a microscopic pattern and with temporal sequences of milliseconds, whose performance is incomparably better apparently than any known physical instrument. Thus mind modifies the spatio-temporal activity of the neuronal network, by exerting spatio-temporal "fields of influence" that become effective through this unique detector function of the active cerebral cortex; and mind is in turn modified by the spatio-temporal activity of the cortex, apparently by having in turn some detector system of its own.

Now with all due respect, this is the merest nonsense. What Eccles is postulating is simply another unknown and unobservable organ of the body, which is a sort of further refinement of the known cortex and its functions—a "ghost cortex", with more minute structures and more microscopic functions. We must face the dilemma; either the mind is mental or physical. If it is mental, it cannot exercise a spatio-temporal field of influence, no matter how minute, whereas if it is physical, it is not mind in the sense in which one poses the problem. Eccles goes to great lengths to avoid materialism but ends with (and I quote) "a mind influence which has a spatio-temporal pattern character." This is only a euphemism for "material", or else our knowledge of physics describes a spirit world.

You will by now have noticed that all formulations of the problem to date depend on the assumption that "this" which you can see and feel and hear is not "me", but that "I" am something hidden away in my own brain, something that could be described as a sort of puff of smoke hovering around the cortex. Now if I suggest that any such concept is false, and that instead, I am living organism, it is likely that to some of you this may sound the rankest heresy and pure materialism. Yet that is the simple truth. Always the problem has appeared in the form: there is a body with its own functions and processes which we can study. There is a mind which we can experience. The body is somehow not really a part of me. I am the mind-thing, and the difficulty is to show some way in which the mind-thing or me can be related to the body and its laws. It seems to me fairly clear that a macroscopic body can have properties and processes which are not observable in or deducible from the elementary particles of which it is composed. It seems to me further that we have all fallen into the trap of thinking that because we can know a truth about something which is not given in immediate experience but arrived at by difficult and devious research, that somehow the truth contained in the latter is about something "more real" than the truth which is more evident. I have no difficulty in granting that this piece of chalk is a mass of spinning electrons with great gaps between its components. But neither have I any difficulty in asserting (and believing it to be true) that this is also a piece of chalk, which I can see, and handle, and with properties which do not come under its physical analysis—such as that I can write with it. In the same way I have no difficulty in accepting that the organism can be made the object of most minute and accurate physico-chemical analysis, so long as nobody is going to deny that the thing which they describe as composed of so many parts in such proportions, is also me. And this macroscopic end-result of the interaction of chemicals has properties which its components have not got. Among other things, it is alive. I do not see that anything is gained by denying that living things differ from non-living things. The fact that their component parts do not differ is no different from saying that both systems belong in the world of matter. Chemistry, physics and physiology do not deny that there are conscious sensations and cognitive reactions. They simply do not deal with them. And whenever a physiologist talks about such phenomena, he does so not as a physiologist but as a psychologist, or as a philosopher. There can be no experimental proof that physiology, and hence physics and chemistry, give the whole truth about man. For from their very terms of reference they deal only with such phenomena of man as have physical aspects. There is no way by which they can arrive at the conclusion that there is no other type of phenomena to be found.

Moreover there are curious contradictions about the physical account of the world and the organism. It is alleged, as we saw earlier, that the physical account of light and the physiologist's account of the organism make it impossible that the end-result in sensation should have any relation other than a casual one with the original source or percept. One can ask, and it is not a trick question: if the end-result is always and necessarily different, how could we ever know that it was? and moreover, it is precisely through such end-results of sensory processes that the physicist and physiologist claim to know both the nature of the stimulus and of the responding mechanisms. They cannot have it both ways.

If our knowledge is always and necessarily different from what we claim to know, then this must hold as much for physics and physiology as for any other object of study. The answer here is not that the physicist or physiologist is wrong in his physics or physiology, but that these specialties are not studies of sensation or consciousness, and to attempt to answer questions about these phenomena in terms of physics and physiology is just as logical as to attempt answers to quantum physics in terms of psychology. One of the sources of trouble seems to be that we assume that we know what knowledge ought to be (apparently some sort of replica of the physical object actually received as a physical thing), and when this is not found to be so, we at once think that our knowledge is defective. This is obvious apriorism and bad scientific method.

It is equally deplorable scientifically, to accept an obvious self-contradiction or "the theoretically impossible", i.e. that the laws of physics are suspended or that a new physics begins to operate when one considers the organism. It is more satisfactory scientifically, and more logical, to accept (a) that this organism you can see and hear and feel is me. I am not something attached to this. (b) That with one single exception, all the processes of this thing you can see are processes of the organism. Sensation is the total response of the organism—not a purely mental content "produced" by the neural processes. Emotion is not a mental thing with physiological consequences. It is the physiological processes. Overactivity of these processes protracted through time will result in physiological symptoms, just as surely as keeping the eye wide open with a bright light flashed into it for too long a time. Psychosomatic medicine is not an account of psychic factors producing physical lesions, but of disorders of a person, who happens to be a psycho-physical unit. Lycergic acid-serotonin imbalance should not be thought of as a physico-chemical cause producing a psychical effect, but rather as a physico-chemical cause affecting a psycho-physical unit. It is not my mind that bends my arm, it is I, a psycho-physical unit, who do so. Will is not a force disposing of physical energy, no matter how tenuous or difficult to detect. It is I, the person, again a psycho-physical unit, who act. It is not the neural mechanism from retina to visual cortex which sees, it is I who see. Light can bleach the visual purple, but the visual purple, no matter how photosensitive, cannot see. Serotonin can antagonize lycergic acid, but it is the person who is ill, and can be cured. Science has always avoided and eliminated where possible, the invocation of "unobservables" to account for its phenomena. The switchboard operator, the puff of smoke around the cortex, are the unobservable. If I make two postulates, both of which are observable, but not in test-tubes, all the phenomena can be accounted for: (a) that living things are somehow different from non-living, (though the difference need not be a chemical one) and (b) that man has one operation (rational thought) which is not psycho-physical, but immaterial, all the complex phenomena we have been considering can be accounted for. But at this point the argument becomes metaphysics: and that is a territory where, as Fred Hoyle says, the scientist at all events will not attempt any answer. Some of the authors referred to above seem to have thought that the most difficult of human problems should have easy answers. There is no *a priori* reason why this should be so.

6 personality and immortality

To philosophize successfully in these days, one must learn
to speak many languages. The words used by the philosophers may very well belong in one or other of the recognized
living languages of educated men. But as used by the philosopher they constitute a private language to the conventions
of which only the initiated are contracting parties. This
makes it difficult for the general reader or intelligent layman
for whom so much contemporary philosophy is allegedly
written. And it means a certain breach of good faith on the
part of the philosopher: for very often he does not bother
to make clear to his general reader the private meanings of
the language he uses. One suspects that sometimes at least
the device of the private language is used as a practical
joke. The reader is being gently or maliciously mocked while
he thinks he is being treated seriously as a philosopher.

The techniques of salesmanship and advertising are more
extensively used in philosophy than one might suppose.
Automobiles are sold in the United States by a gimmick
called "psychological obsolescence": one does not need a new
car, one's current car is perfectly good still, but one simply
cannot go on driving it for another year; it is psychologically obsolete. This is perhaps the most common device used

in philosophy at the moment. One does not argue the merits of a case. One simply asserts that the opposite is obsolete.

As an example, consider the following well-known passage from Bertrand Russell: ". . . The Aristotelian doctrines (of logic, which he has just expounded) are wholly false, with the exception of the formal theory of the syllogism which is unimportant. Any person in the present day who wishes to learn logic will be wasting his time if he reads Aristotle or any of his disciples." (*History of Western Philosophy*, 1946). The possibility of an alternative point of view is not even suggested, and it is extremely unlikely that many of the readers of Russell's popular history will also read Sir David Ross, for example, or Lukasiewicz, or even a lesser light like Sinclair of Edinburgh. I quote from the fifth edition (1951, reprinted 1954) of Sinclair's *Traditional Fomal Logic*: "What logic is, and why it is worth studying, are difficult to understand until we are reasonably familiar with the variety of it known as the traditional formal logic." Later, in the same vein, he speaks of its "unique importance", it is "an educational essential", it is of "surpassing importance", and "all the other logical theories that have been and are being advanced have arisen out of the traditional doctrine, either by extension of it, or by disagreement with it, varying from minor criticism to total rejection". All these quotations are from the first two pages of Sinclair's work. But there is not a hint of the possibility of this point of view in Russell. I do not suggest that Sinclair is as great a logician as Russell. That is not the point at issue. The point is that the general reader is misled by his own lack of knowledge of the background of any given philosophical problem, and by the technique of some authors in presenting their own point of view as if it were the only tenable one.

The point can be made in another way. Why should it be

acceptable for Russell to suggest that St. Thomas is "insincere" (*loc. cit.,* p.484), but intolerable to suggest that perhaps this might apply to Russell too? "The finding of arguments for a conclusion given in advance is not philosophy, but special pleading", says Russell, speaking of St. Thomas's philosophy (p.485). It would be interesting should this prove to be the case with Russell himself.

In his article on the possibility of survival after death (*Sunday Times,* January 6, 1957), Russell appeals to Hume. He quotes with evident approval the well-known passage in Part IV, Section VI of the *Treatise of Human Nature.* The passage runs: "For my part, when I enter most intimately into what I might call myself, I always stumble on some particular perception or other, of heat or cold, light or shade, love or hatred, pain or pleasure. I never can catch myself at any times without a perception, and never can observe anything but the perception." What Russell did not explain, and probably could not be expected to explain within the confines of Sunday journalism, was the point at issue in this passage, and the premises assumed by Hume which determined his outlook not in this problem alone but on all philosophical issues. The point at issue is given by Hume in the opening words of the section: "There are some philosophers who imagine we are every moment intimately conscious of what we call our self; that we feel its existence and its continuance in existence; and are certain, beyond the evidence of a demonstration, both of its perfect identity and simplicity." Hume had in mind the Cartesians, and particularly Descartes himself. And there is no doubt that Hume in the passage quoted is right. We do not find a direct awareness of self in any introspectible act of consciousness.

This sometimes strikes people as odd, because they have long thought that they had a direct awareness of themselves.

St. Thomas argued that a direct awareness of oneself of this kind is the prerogative of the Divine Intellect, whereas the human intellect *intelligit seipsum per speciem intelligibilem, sicut et alia.* In modern English, this is the assertion that our conscious awareness of ourselves is through conceptual constructions formed in the same way as we form them about anything else. And this means forming them by intellectual processes whereby we use the data of sense to achieve nonsensory intellectual contents. Of what then are we directly aware? Always of some act or content of consciousness: in Hume's terminology, we are aware of some perception of heat or cold, light or shade, love or hatred, etc. But Hume had already ruled out the possibility of there being any mental content other than sensory (and Russell knew this). Hume was well versed in the thought of Berkeley, who had recently ("of late years" is Hume's phrase) denied that there were or could be any such things as abstract ideas. Hume claims this denial of Berkeley's as "one of the greatest and most valuable discoveries. ..."

It is not difficult, in the light of the foregoing paragraph, to translate the passage quoted approvingly by Russell, from Hume's private language into contemporary English. It would then read: "My introspective knowledge of myself does not reveal anything corresponding to the Cartesian self. I cannot discover any abstract ideas as these are normally understood ('according to the common method of explaining them' - Part I, Section VII. Does this mean a denial of Cartesian innate ideas? If so, Hume is right to that extent). All I can ever discover is a sensory content."

It is unlikely that anyone would quarrel with Hume's denial of the Cartesian self or the Cartesian "clear and distinct ideas", including the idea of the "self". But there are many who would question the last assertion: that all I can ever discover is a sensory content. The evidence of experiment is that there exist "contents of consciousness" which are not sensory in character. These are the Bewusstseinslagen of the German psychologists who labored in the laboratory of Wurzburg for ten years to study them. Few psychologists would now make the claim of Hume, and this for two reasons. First, because of the experimental evidence in regard to consciousness; and second, because of the increased understanding of the unconscious. Hume could not introspect the unconscious, nor can anybody else, and yet it would be rash to deny its existence, its contents and its functions. But there is no reference to these matters in Russell's article. We shall return to the point in a moment in considering the notion of memory, and the sweeping assertion of Russell "that the most essential thing in the continuity of a person is memory".

Russell claims to examine the belief in survival "from a purely scientific point of view". This seems to have impressed many readers. The purely scientific point of view means, I take it, the point of view which claims (a) that it is going to study only observable phenomena, (b) by the methods of observation and experiment. From this point of view it is unscientific to ignore, as Russell does, the experimental and clinical evidence about mind. Moreover, the scientific point of view means the adoption of a methodology which at once rules out the possibility of studying certain kinds of problems: the nature of beauty or moral goodness, for example. And if there are disembodied spirits or angels, they will be forever by definition beyond the range of study from the "purely scientific point of view" simply because, not being material in any way, they will not be "observable phenomena". But the fact that something is unobservable does not mean that it does not exist. If one accepts the proposition "that whatever is not observable sensorially does not exist", then of course the conclusion will follow. But the proposition that "whatever is not observable sensorially does not exist" is not only not known to be true, but could not be shown to be true. In other words it is not a scientific proposition, but a dogmatic assumption. Yet it is assumed by Hume and also by Russell.

But Russell's argument depends on his doctrine about memory. "The most essential thing," he tells us, "in the continuity of a person is memory." This has a specious plausibility. It will be true if I state it as follows: "The most essential thing in the awareness of continuity of a person is memory." But this is a radically different proposition. It means for example that a person suffering from total amnesia will not be aware of his continuity as a person—he will have "forgotten who he was". This is not at all an impossibility—it happens frequently enough. Yet no one, not even Russell, I think, would deny that in total amnesia the patient is still, in a perfectly intelligible sense, the same person that he was before his loss of memory. But in terms of Russell's formulation this would not be so. The awareness of continuity as a person is not at all the same thing, logically or psychologically, as continuity as a person. Russell concludes: "We may therefore take memory as what defines the continuity of a person." The "therefore" is good, as it suggests that something has been proved.

The argument from memory, however, can be shown by a simple tour de force to establish a concluson which flatly contradicts Russell's conclusion. The argument would take the following form: I can remember something which happened to me twenty years ago. (This would hardly be denied, even by Russell.) But if this be so, then I must have had a continuous existence since the event I claim to remember happened. But it cannot be the organism alone which is responsible for this continuous existence, since biologists tell me that all the cells of my organism are different from those which constituted me twenty years ago. Therefore "I" am somehow a persistent entity, even though the organism is constantly changing. But Russell rejects this persistent entity. It will be helpful to consder this a while longer.

The argument is Hume's, and runs as follows: "I venture to affirm of the rest of mankind that they are nothing but a bundle or collection of different perceptions, which succeed each other with an inconceivable rapidity, and are in a perpetual flux or movement. . . . The mind is a kind of theater, where several perceptions make their appearance; pass, repass; glide away and mingle in an infinite variety of postures and situations. . . ." But he warns that "the comparison of the theater must not mislead us": there is really no state nor any theater at all, but only the succession of scenes. There is no "mind" or "self", but only the succession of mental contents. Hume makes due allowance for anyone "who has a different notion", and says: "All I can allow him is that he may be in the right as well as I"; but Russell makes no such concession. He gives the impression au contraire, that what he says is scientifically established. Now with regard to Hume's argument, if we speak in terms of the pure experience of consciousness, he is right. That is to say, that as far as experience goes, the literal account of mind must be of a series of mental states or contents or processes. But it was long ago pointed out by Bradley that Hume's conception of mind was incomplete. It was a hank of self-supporting onions on a non-existent rope. And many philosophers pointed out the philosophical problem which this conception posed but did not answer. If the mind is simply the succession of its own states, then how can it become conscious of itself as a succession of states? For all earlier states have ceased to exist before this present state of my mind. The series does not exist, but only the momentary term in the series. And it is not profitable to appeal to memory; since by definition mind is only the succession of its states, it must be the present state which remembers all the others. But the present state is by definition only a mental event or content. How can one mental event or content be said to "know" or "remember" another? much less to remember a whole series? and at the same time to account for consciousness and self-consciousness?

Philosophers, like other men, have minds. They are subject to some at least of the defense-mechanisms revealed in analysis: repression, dissociation—perhaps more than any other, they are subject to rationalization. John Stuart Mill understood this argument of Hume's and the difficulty of a series becoming conscious of itself as a series. But at least he faced the issue squarely as a scientist should. It was self-contradictory, he thought, that a series should thus become conscious of itself, but he preferred to accept the contradiction rather than the consequence: a substantial persistent entity through time. For this would at once pose the question about the nature of this substantial persistent entity. It is unlikely that Russell is unaware of this problem. But many of his readers will not have heard of it, while scientific integrity would seem to demand that it should be made clear to them.

Russell goes on: "The question whether we survive death thus becomes the question: Are there, after a man dies, memories of what happened to him while he lived on earth?" It is perhaps trivial to point out the inconsequential "thus" in this sentence. But it is more to the point to examine the question itself. The question presumably does not mean: Does anybody remember what happened to so-and-so while he lived on earth? For this question can certainly be answered in the affirmative without prejudice to any question about survival. The question therefore must mean something else. It might mean: After a man dies, does he remember what happened to him while he lived on earth? But this is no advance over the question: does man survive death (except perhaps in this sense, that survival might be possible without self-consciousness, and therefore without memory, as would appear to be the Buddhist view: but this possibility is ruled out in advance for Russell because of his identification of personality with memory). The question thus becomes: Do disembodied memories occur as a series through time?

The apparent simplicity of this question is deceptive. It might mean: do disembodied memories occur through time, with nobody who has these memories? Or it might mean: do disembodied memories occur through time with nobody who is these memories? The first form of the question does not arise for Russell, since in any case there is nobody who has memories—memories are the person who thinks he has them. This is clear from paragraph 2 of his article: "A critical enquiry does not reveal the existence of any such persistent entity as the core of the personality", where the words "persistent entity" refer to "soul", "mind", "self", or "subject". The second form of the question is more important. If disembodied memories occur through time, even though nobody has these memories, they would automatically constitute a person on Russell's premises. Russell's task therefore seems a simple one. He has only to show that there are not memories in order to show that there is no survival after death. Up to this point he seems to be using the word "memories" in an ordinary "public" sense to refer to mental events and contents. In any reasonable public use of language, one would reason as follows: Memories are either composed of matter or they are not so composed. They are either self-supporting or they are not self-supporting. Russell agrees (paragraph 9) that "thoughts and feelings are evanescent", and it is precisely on this ground that philosophers argue that these are not self-supporting but demand a subject. In order to avoid this conclusion, Russell falls back on the assertion that thoughts and feelings "compose the brain". As the brain is clearly material by any definition, it would seem to follow that thoughts and feelings (of which memories are a species) will have to be material. But at this point the argument reverts to a private language: "When I mention the brain in this connection, I shall expect to be accused of materialism. This accusation, however, would be unjust." But it is extremely difficult to see how in the usage of any public language this is not materialism. In fact, the identification of thoughts and feelings with the brain is only a surreptitious way of re-introducing the notion of "self" or "subject", but in materialistic terms.

Russell is one of the ablest thinkers of the century, and one of the five or six greatest logicians of all time. From the purely scientific point of view, he is open to the criticism that he has not taken account of all the evidence. From the logical point of view, he has attempted to establish an universal negative proposition—which notoriously can only be done by deduction from another universal negative. And the one universal negative on which Russell's argument depends ("whatever is not experienced by the senses does not exist") cannot be established.

From the psychological point of view, Russell's argument amounts to saying that people believe in survival because of their fears and their wishes. Even if fears or wishes accounted for belief in survival, as they might very well do for many people, the question of survival itself remains to be answered. This is the fallacy of historicism: the fallacy of thinking that because we can explain historically why a particular belief is held, therefore the content of the belief is false. Freud committed this fallacy in connection with the existence of God, and there are many other examples of it, particularly in anthropology, comparative religion, the Higher Criticism and sociology.

Philosophically, Russell's article is a good example of finding reasons for a belief held independently of the reasons given for it. Psychologists call this rationalization.

The argument for survival is extremely complex, and in a summary exposition would certainly be unconvincing. Scotus in fact characterized all rational argument for immortality as merely probable, and fell back on faith. But St. Thomas thought it could be proved. The argument depends on (a) the relation between action and agent, (b) the nature of the soul, (c) the relation between matter and spirit, leading to the notion of possibility of survival. From possibility to actual survival, the argument takes two steps: one consists in showing that the soul does not by natural means cease to be; the other, in showing that God does not annihilate it. The question of resurrection and bodily survival should not be confused with the question of survival. Resurrection and bodily survival are matters of revealed faith. But the possibility and fact of immortality, though difficult, are matters that reason can and should tackle. For, as Gabriel Marcel puts it, "the problem of immortality is the pivot of metaphysic".

It is fairly obvious that if there is no such thing as "soul", there can be no such thing as immortality. One could still urge and reason about the "eternity" of matter but the eternity of matter, either backwards or forwards in time, is irrelevant to the question: do I survive the death of the body?

The problem of the eternity of the world, in so far as reason can cope with it, can be put very simply. Since God always is, in an eternal *nunc,* the act of creation of a finite universe (speaking anthropomorphically) could have occurred at any "point" in God's existence, or could have been "coterminous" with the existence of God. The fact that this was not the case is not known from reason but from revelation. The possibility of eternity "forwards" in time follows from the difference between transformation and annihilation. Transformations of matter are familiar. Hydrogen and oxygen "become" or are "changed into" water. There is a loss of energy; but it is not simply reduced to nothingness. The energy is taken up by something else.

The notion of nothingness is difficult. It is not just a blank surrounded by something else, as one might think when considering the possibility of a perfect vacuum. There is no known instance of "reduction to nothingness" in the physical world, any more than there is of creation. But the loose and inaccurate use of the word "annihilation" in connection with atomic energy has led the public to think that matter is literally "annihilated" or reduced to nothingness. In fact it is converted into energy, and energy is still a phenomenon of the physical material world. The loose use of "annihilation" is paralleled by the equally loose use of the word "creation" e.g. by Fred Hoyle, who thinks that matter is being "eternally created" when what he means apparently is that energy is constantly being transformed into "matter".

There is no known instance of annihilation (in the literal sense) in the physical universe. Appeals to thermodynamics will not help: entropy may mean the cessation of all movement and change, but it is not the same as "ceasing to be". Nor does it help to speculate on the possibility of a bomb superior to the H-bomb, of such power, or instigating a chain reaction of such magnitude, that our universe would be "annihilated". For, once again, the position is that our universe would be converted into something else: energy, perhaps, but I leave that to the physicists. Such an event might be the end of "our world", but not necessarily the end of "the world". We must take it that, as far as human reason can penetrate the problem, matter could be eternal. Annihilation is the prerogative of divine power, the correlation of creation.

If it is assumed, as Russell seems to assume, that man is nothing but matter, then his "eternity" will follow from the eternity of matter itself. But of course, Russell would agree that his continuity as a person would cease. The continuing in existence of the atoms or particles of which I am composed is not at all the same as my continuing in existence. It seems that if Russell wished to be completely consistent, his argument could have been stated in a few sentences: "I am nothing but a collection of elementary particles organized in a particular way. It is manifest that this organization breaks down. But the particles go on existing. This is not immortality. But there is nothing else. Therefore there is no immortality". But the concepts of me, ego, self, person, are hard to get rid of. Consciousness and mental life are equally difficult to get rid of. Hence the inevitable falling back on a discussion of memory and continuity, rather than a straight statement of the materialist hypothesis.

The "reduction" of man to a group of elementary particles or, more generally, the elimination of any difference between living and non-living matter has become a habitual mode of thought with many. Sherrington (*Man on His Nature*), though he does not subscribe to this doctrine, states it very well. Referring to a well-known passage where Eddington speaks of his table and his elbow resting on it, Sherrington says:

> "True, there is between the elbow and the table the difference that the one is 'living' and the other is dead. Chemistry and physics say nothing of this. Or rather they say a great deal about it, but do not in saying it make use of either of these words. If we tell them that the table was at one time living wood and is now dead wood, that the wood was at one time part of a living tree, they do not recognize the word as conveying any radical distinction between the two.... Chemistry says that neither in the one case nor in the other does it find anything or any behavior which is not chemical."

And again Pirenne (*British Journal for the Philosophy of Science*, 11, 8) makes an important point: "An examination of physics qua physics gives no indication that the new physical laws should not apply to the components of the human body." But neither does Pirenne accept the materialist hypothesis. It would be interesting, but perhaps unprofitable, to compile a list of quotations from Eddington, Hinshelwood, Adrian, each of whom in his own way states the problem and rejects the materialist hypothesis, very often, as with Sherrington, by doing violence to his own scientific thinking. Sherrington is prepared to accept the theoretically impossible, as he puts it: that is to say, he accepts the physico-chemical account of man, the reality of mind, the impossibility that mind and matter should affect one another, but accepts in addition that in fact they do so. This would appear to be the position of many contemporaries—a sort of reversion to an Averroist "double-truth" theory.

The way out of the apparent impasse depends on hard

philosophical thinking. The impasse derives from what Ryle
has called the "Official Doctrine", "Descartes' Myth", "the
dogma of the Ghost in the Machine". This myth he derives
not only from Descartes, but also from "Scholastic and
Reformation theology", "Stoic-Augustinian theories of the
will", "Platonic and Aristotelian theories of the intellect"
(*The Concept of Mind*, 1949, page 23). Reasoning better
than he realized, he reverted to what is in essence (though
not in detail or in the consequences he draws from it) a good
thomistic concept of man as one being. St. Thomas's problem
was not: how is soul as spirit related to a body existing in
its own right so that the product is man? This was Plato,
St. Augustine, Scotus, Descartes and I fear many who would
even still claim to follow St. Thomas's teaching. But rather:
given that this being, sitting or standing in front of me, is
Socrates, how is it that the following propositions can all
be true about him at the same time: he weighs 180 lbs., he
is subject to the law of gravity, he grows, he sees, he feels,
he thinks? In philosophical terms this is the problem: how
is it that one and the same being can sustain apparently
contradictory predicates—he is matter, he is spirit?

The solution of Plato and the others listed above consisted
always in saying: there is no contradiction. He is really two
beings, and some of these predicates are true of one of
these beings and others are true of the other. But St. Thomas
will have none of this. Perhaps his greatest, but certainly
his most controversial, contribution to the philosophy of the
middle ages was his rejection. long before Ryle, of the dogma
of the ghost in the machine.

His solution is a psycho-physical composite, neither of
whose components is a complete being: the same kind of
composition which is found in every other creature in the
physical universe, a composition between a formal and a

material principle. But this must not be thought of as a simple combination of "organization" with "elementary particles". It is a metaphysical union of principles of being. This is not an out-moded solution but a previously misunderstood one. The theory of elementary particles in no wise upsets it. For if there really are elementary particles, they will be themselves so composed. And if there are not (Schroedinger apparently thought there were not: see "Are there Elementary Particles?", *Endeavour*, 1950; *Brit. Jour. Phil. Science*, 1952. Dingle has called them "physical symbols", and most physicists think of them apparently as conceptual constructions; but the public does not know this), they cannot upset the theory of co-principles of being.

It is not my intention to engage in a dispute with modern physics. But a word on this problem may not be out of place here since it is often contended that modern physics, and especially its applications in cybernetics, had radically altered the problems involved in a philosophy of man. It is worth noting that this has not happened through pronouncements of the great physicists, but rather through the popularized versions which the public has access to. Thus, in spite of many disclaimers on the part of all the great physicists, many still believe the billiard-ball analogy of the atom, and many who would reject this in the case of the atom appear to cling to it still in endeavoring to understand the elementary particles. It is assumed by many that these particles are durable little things with individuality, and that we are composed of such "little things". But Schroedinger laid down categorically that "(a particle) is not a durable little thing with individuality" (*Brit. Jour. Phil. Science*, 1952). According to Max Born, who described this viewpoint as "reactionary", Schroedinger has, "right from the beginning", taken the view that "there are no particles, no stationary states, and no transitions" (1953). Schroedinger in fact went even further: there are not even "waves"; "The waves are not quite real waves": "Whatever meaning we may give to the dangerous epithet 'real', all quantitative models or images conceived by the physicist are, epistemologically, only mathematical devices for computing observable events. . . ."

The explanatory value of elementary particles is of course beyond question, and one can only admire and be grateful to the physicists for their achievements. But in sheer logic, it should be pointed out that a concept or set of concepts which "explain" something are not thereby shown to have an ontological counterpart. "Phlogiston" and "ether" are classical examples of concepts which appeared for a time to "explain" phenomena, but which were subsequently abandoned for lack of any reality corresponding. Some "explanatory concepts" are "logical fictions". Russell instances geometrical points and instants of time, but there are others. The cycles and epicycles of Ptolemaic astronomy turned out to be logical fictions, and "the unconscious" in contemporary psychology will be seen on reflection to be a good example of an "explanatory concept" which, however convinced one might be of its reality, might turn out to be a logical fiction. For the independent demonstration of its existence turns out to be "impossible by definition".

It is true that most physicists tend to eschew the Schroedinger articles, but then it is also true that most physicists prescind from any discussion of the "real existence" of elementary particles. Their position appears to be expressible in some such form as this: "Something" exists, and these are the explanatory concepts which render it intelligible and (to some extent) controllable. This statement is in no sense intended as a reflection on physics or physicists, but only to show that, in spite of *a priori* assumptions to the contrary, the elementary particles do not raise new philosophical problems in the philosophy of man. For it was always clear (except perhaps to panpsychists) that the organism is material—so that whatever is true of matter will be true of the organism.

The fact that the organism is subject to the law of gravity but that "thought" is not so subject raises the same philosophical problems as are raised by cybernetics or the quantum theory. For the problem is: how can this one individual being, man, or Socrates, whose organism is material (whatever matter is), be also at one and the same time a "thinking thing"? The term "thinking thing" is of course Descartes' term, but it is used here without prejudice to the theories of Descartes. The watershed which divides all philosophies of man is found right here. For either one assumes that "matter" can think, or that it cannot. The fact of thinking is indisputable, but the assumption that matter can think can only be made either by a purely verbal supposition or by ignoring the nature of thinking itself. One could never explain what thinking is to a being who did not already know in some way what thinking is, since the very fact of explanation involves a conscious cognitive receptive being, who already knows something and moreover knows that it knows. It is easy of course to make suppositions and to suppose that thought is something other than thought: e.g., that it is an electronic process in a complex machine. But all attempts at "reducing" thought to non-cognitive elements will prove unsatisfactory as long as the person who makes the supposition retains conscious awareness, that is, as long as he "knows that he knows". A little reflection will show that this line of speculation will lead to the conclusion that whatever the relation of psychological functions to physiological factors, they are not the same as the physiological factors.

Just as there could be no immortality if there were no soul, so also there could be no immortality if the soul had not already a real existence of its own, or if it were composed of whatever matter is composed of. For the only "immortality" of matter is the tenuous possible "eternity" of its parts, and something which is dependent for its existence on a particular organization of matter or material particles cannot survive the disintegration of such organization. The fact that matter as such does not "think" but that man in fact "thinks" is the basis of the argument which establishes the required propositions about soul, viz., that it has real existence of its own and that it is not composed of matter.

With regard to the possibility of survival after death, there is an interesting reflection to be made. It is very often asserted in connection with the question "can matter think?" that whereas we know a great deal about what matter can do, any assertion about what it cannot do must be invalid on grounds of apriorism. The assertion that the soul cannot survive the body can be countered by the same reasoning: we know a great deal about the soul and what it can do, but any assertion about what it cannot do (e.g., that it cannot survive the body) must be invalid on the grounds of apriorism. But those who put forward the former argument are not inclined to accept the latter, even though the logic of both is the same; or they are tempted to fall back on a simple agnosticism, protesting that they do not know. I am not suggesting that either argument is valid, but only that consistency demands the acceptance or rejection of both. The latter does not establish immortality (or even the possibility of it) any more than the former establishes the fact or possibility that matter can think. But it has a specious plausibility. The assertion that matter cannot think does not depend simply on what we do not know about matter, but rather on what we do know about thought.

The possibility of survival can be established fairly directly. If the soul is what we have been contending it is, viz., something with an existence of its own and an activity of its own (thought), and is not an organization of matter, it will be seen that it could continue to exist: for these three assertions add up to the notion of immaterial substance. There is no way of establishing this "scientifically" (in Russell's sense of the word). But it is worth recalling that the logic of the thinking involved is the same as that of the scientist who investigates matter. For he infers from the observable (e.g., the tracks on a photographic plate) to the unobservable (the inner constitution of matter); just as the philosopher infers from the observable (the behavior of man, including thought) to the unobservable (immaterial substance).

The notion of immaterial substance is foreign both to the scientific mind and the empiricist philosopher. Yet the scientific mind (as witness: Sherrington, Adrian, Hinshelwood, Eddington, Einstein and others) finds it easier to accept (even if for the wrong reasons) than does the empiricist philosopher. Compare, for example, Hinshelwood and Ayer. In an essay entitled "Chemistry and Modern Thought" (1953) Professor Sir Cyril Hinshelwood, F.R.S., says: "It may reasonably be said that a purely materialist attitude (to 'the age-old problem of the relation of mind and matter') seems rather more hopeless than ever ..."; and in a larger work (1951) he appeals to the thomistic theory of angels to illustrate a point about the internal construction of the atom. Professor Ayer on the other hand, in his *The Problem of Knowledge* (1956), finds the notion of spiritual substance unintelligible. "A view which I have not considered is that people are differentiated from one another . . . by being different spiritual substances, or souls. And the reason why I have not considered it is that I do not find it intelligible." (Page 209.) But this statement of his is not really very good philosophizing, since "intelligible" has a technical meaning in Ayer (it means something like "capable of withstanding the sort of test which would apply to sensory experience"— but that is my own phrase, not Professor Ayer's). And we have already stated that by definition, as it were, this sort of test could not apply. The second reason why Ayer's statement is not very good philosophizing is that to say that one does not find something to be intelligible may very well be a statement about oneself, not about that which is said to be unintelligible.

The question: "does this immaterial (or 'spiritual') substance actually survive the death of the body?" cannot be answered by experiment. And it can be answered in the negative either by a *nego suppositum* argument or by a statement of impossibility. The *nego suppositum* argument would run: "By asking the question, you are supposing that there is such a thing as a spiritual substance. But I deny your supposition. Therefore there is no actual survival." The discussion thereupon ceases to be a discussion about immortality and reverts to one about the possibility of there being spiritual substances.

The second form the answer might take is this: "It is impossible that anything should exist apart from matter. Therefore, even if there is a spiritual component in man (but in fact, the argument would usually but not necessarily go on, there is not) it could not survive the death of the body." This could very well have been the thinking of the Sadducees, or the Greeks with whom St. Paul contended in the Areopagus: *cum audissent autem resurrectionem mortuorum, quidam quidem irridebant*... (Acts. 17). This argument clearly depends on the assertion that it is impossible that anything should exist apart from matter. But there is no way in which this proposition could be shown to be true. Either it must be assumed dogmatically (which is not good empiricism) or else some proposition which implies it must be assumed. The usual empiricist assumption which is alleged to imply the required proposition is of the form: only what is given in sensory experience exists. This in fact is the essence of empiricism. But neither can it be shown to be true, since there is no sensory test which could possibly be appealed to in order to establish it; and yet a sensory test is the only sort of test allowed in empiricism.

Instead of asking the question in the form "does the soul survive the body?" it can be asked in the form: "does the soul cease to be?" and in this form it becomes much more manageable. For if one can state the ways in which things cease to be, and then show that these do not apply to the soul it will follow that it does not cease to be, i.e., that it is immortal. It is important to remember, however, that there is an enormous difference between a thing's ceasing to be, on the one hand, and its ceasing to be what it is, on the other. Our only experience of "ceasing to be" is in fact the experience of things ceasing to be what they are. That is to say, we experience change, transformation, resolution into parts, reduction to elements, molecules, atoms, or particles. The argument that the soul does not cease to be has a deductive or *a priori* appearance in the form in which it is usually presented, because it is usually presented in a truncated form. In fact it is essentially an inductive piece of reasoning on the basis of experience.

There is one further point: a thing can cease to be red,

or blue, or hot or cold, or large or small, without ceasing either to be or to be what it is. This kind of ceasing-to-be certainly applies to the soul: it ceases to be conscious, or to be actively engaged in thinking or feeling, etc. But this is clearly not the kind of ceasing to be which is intended in the question of survival—unless one accepts the Humean doctrine examined in a former chapter: the doctrine which claims that the soul is nothing but a series of such experiences. But this we have already, in the chapter referred to, found to be inadequate. On the other hand, this kind of ceasing-to-be can help or clear up one difficulty. If the soul were in the same sort of category as "red", "large", or "hot", if it were a mere quality or quantity or in general an "accident" of the body, then it would be subject to this kind of ceasing-to-be. There were in fact some nineteenth century philosophers who took this line, and described soul (or more usually "mind") as an epiphenomenon of the brain. This would still be the point of view, though the terminology might be different, of those who think that electronic brains can "think". But this means in fact that there is no soul, and if there is no soul there cannot be an immortal soul. Consequently, dealing with this point of view one is not really dealing with immortality, but the larger issue of materialism.

There is another obvious fact about accidents: they can cease to be with the destruction of their "host". Thus the "shape" of the statue ceases to exist with the destruction of the statue. If the soul were an accident of the body, it could cease to be in some way as this; but then it is not an accident of the body; it is something which has existence and functions of its own. This is clearly not true of the shape of the statue: it has no existence in its own right, and there is nothing it can do of itself. One can of course deny the possibility of immaterial (or "spiritual") substance as we have seen, but the assertion: "there are no spiritual substances" is incapable of proof. And the denial itself involves the denial of immortality. Consequently, the issue once again is not really the issue of immortality, but the antecedent question of the possibility of spiritual substance.

With regard to things other than accidents, the things for instance which are either red or blue or hot or cold, we have already made the assertion that such things do not cease to be in an absolute sense, but only by becoming something else, cease to be what they are. The difference is enormous. It is the difference between essence and existence, between infinite and finite causes, between reduction to parts and reduction to nothingness. With regard to anything which is composed of parts, reduction to its component parts is possible. If there are no parts, such reduction is impossible. The history of the atom illustrates the point clearly. As long as the atom was regarded as the "ultimate" constituent of matter, it was also regarded as irreducible. This is why the "splitting of the atom" seemed to be such an exciting achievement. For the splitting of the atom meant that it was composed of parts (however such composition is to be understood) and meant also, therefore, the abandoning of the supposition that it was an ultimate particle, with consequential recasting of our ideas about matter.

The soul is not composed of parts, has no dimensions, is not quantitative in any way, so that reduction to constituent parts does not arise. The soul has different kinds of functions and different kinds of capacity for carrying out such functions, but a capacity (e.g., intellect) is not a component part but an ability to act in a particular way. This is what is technically called the "simplicity" of the soul, a term which in English can be misleading. But *simplex* as opposed to complex carries no such misleading connotations. Complex means composed of parts, but *simplicitas* (from *simplex*) is the quality or property of not having parts. The *simplicitas* of the soul follows from its not being composed of whatever matter is composed of, nor is it a composition of matter and something else. For the former would mean that it was incapable of thought while the latter simply leads to an infinite regress: if there were such a composition, it is the "something else", not the matter in the composition, which would be the soul; and if this something else is so composed, then again the soul will be the non-material constituent, and so on.

The conclusion must be that the soul does not cease to be by reduction to parts. And the only alternative remaining for consideration is the possibility of ceasing to be outright; this means annihilation, and the term is used here literally. Does the soul cease to be by its being reduced to nothingness, to non-existence, by an exercise of omnipotent power? Annihilation is the correlative of creation. The latter means causing something to be where there was nothing; the former is the reverse process; and neither is within the compass of finite beings. If God does not annihilate the soul, then it does not cease to be. Does he do so?

There is no doubt that God could, in his omnipotent power, annihilate the soul. But that he does not do so and will not do so, follows from our knowledge of God, even such knowledge as can be achieved by natural reason without recourse to revelation. For (bearing in mind the difference between finite and infinite, and therefore that our terms are to some extent anthropomorphic, or more accurately are used "analogically") it can be shown that God is intellect. He does not therefore act without a purpose. He therefore had a purpose in making the soul the kind of thing it is: a spiritual substance, not composed of parts, and therefore not subject to the kind of ceasing-to-be to which other creatures are subject. In other words, he made the soul immortal, and he had a purpose in so doing. If now he annihilates the soul, we are faced with a dilemma: either God had no purpose in creating the soul immortal, or he now defeats his own purpose. And both consequents are absurd in regard to God. Therefore the soul is not annihilated. Therefore it is immortal.

One must bear in mind the difference between proving a conclusion and winning assent to it. This was Newman's problem in his *Grammar of Assent*. It is quite clear that people assent to the immortality of the soul for reasons other than philosophical ones. But when it is contended that reason cannot establish a proposition or, as with Russell, that it establishes its contradictory, it becomes imperative to try once again to vindicate reason. The problem of immortality is the pivot of metaphysic (Marcel's words) in the sense that one's stand on this problem determines one's stand on all problems of life. Russell in one of his rare emotional passages falls back on a romantic but perhaps unconvincing Stoicism when he contemplates death: "One by one, as they march, our comrades vanish from our sight, seized by the silent orders of omnipotent Death. Very brief is the time in which we can help them, in which their happiness or misery is decided. Be it ours to shed sunshine on their path, to lighten their sorrows by the balm of sympathy, to give them the pure joy of a never-tiring affection. . . . Let us remember that they are fellow-sufferers in the same darkness, actors in the same darkness, actors in the same tragedy with ourselves. . . ."

The notion that life is a tragedy is echoed in existentialist writings: life is absurd, and angoisse is the key to it. It does not matter what you do, since there are no values, no standards, no criteria, by which to judge the value of life or action.

You create your own values, in your very strivings for purposes, and whatever purpose you choose gives value to your endeavors to attain it. In the long run, however, you are deceived. The malignant demon of death catches up with you, and destroys both your ends and the means you have taken to achieve them. What matters is neither the ends nor the means you have adopted: they are in themselves valueless anyway. What matters is that you should commit yourself wholeheartedly to your ends and means: *engagement totale* is the clue. If you are going to be a murderer, be a clever one; a swindler, be a successful one; a traitor, live for treason. The strength of the existentialist movement in philosophy lies in its consistent logic: in its not flinching from drawing the conclusions to which its premises point. Sartre himself described it as an attempt to draw all the conclusions of consistent atheism. But many, like Russell, try to have it both ways: to retain atheism and materialism, and at the same time to defend traditional values, even ethical ones. It has often been pointed out that on the materialist hypothesis there can be no values, and Kant even went as far as trying to prove the immortality of the soul by a transcendental deduction from the existence of ethical values. At least this much is true: ethical values would be in the long run meaningless without the concept of immortality.

7 freedom, responsibility and guilt

The problem of freedom, responsibility and guilt has been bedevilled for centuries by our habit of forgetting that we are considering the behavior of human beings, and not that of either angels or irrational animals.

It is extremely difficult to rid our minds of the influence of Plato, and of the ideas of Descartes and Leibniz. Platonism (by which I mean here any form of the theory of a spiritual substance dwelling in an organism which is complete in its own right as an organism) is not Christianity, though it is difficult to express the Christian concept of soul and spirit in popular language other than Platonic. (Perhaps we might say that the problem for Christianity is not: how can soul and body be united, but rather, how can they be separated?). To Descartes we owe the conception of man as an essentially conscious *spiritual* being; to Leibniz, the idea of will as a wholly free *disposer of energy* in a vacuum; liberty of equilibrium, free from cause, motive, or intelligibility.

Will is not a pendulum swinging in a vacuum; it is not an auxiliary engine on a yacht; it is not a source of physical energy, in any sense, nor does it dispose arbitrarily of energy already existing in the world. It is not even a source of "psychic" energy, which is a misnomer. Energy is a physical concept, and is applied to mind or psyche or soul, only by analogy.

I think it would help to try to state first what we are concerned with. We are concerned with a sort of Cartesian Ego, dwelling inside our cranium and merely observing what goes on: processes which it does not initiate, direct or control, but merely registers. Such a concept is not even phenomenologically correct. Not only was this the Cartesian Ego, it was also the Humean one. As far as one can judge, it remains a sort of inarticulate concept in the minds of most psychologists who talk about these problems. Let me therefore state that we are the living organism, not something dwelling in the living organism. Everything that the living organism does or can do can be subsumed under the concept of behavior. Behavior therefore I shall use to name each and every process carried out by an organism, other than such processes as are accountable for by the fact that the organism is a physical entity in a physical world (thus, it is subject to gravity, and will "fall" if left unsupported in mid-air. This would hardly be considered "behavior", since it is a process which is due not to the fact that the body is an organism, but to the fact that it is a body). Within the genus "behavior" one finds a certain type of activity which merits the name "conduct". Conduct is that sector of behavior which is ego-initiated, ego-directed, or ego-permitted. The problem of freedom refers to the sector of behavior called conduct. Or more simply, all processes that a physical body undergoes merely because it is a physical body and all processes that occur to an organism or in an organism merely because it is an organism, lie outside the range of freedom. The question is therefore: are there any sectors of behavior which are not wholly accounted for by the fact that I belong in a physical world as a physical body, or by the fact that I am

a living organism; is there, in other words, a sector of behavior which merits the name "conduct"?

There are a few preliminary points that must be clarified.
I shall state a number of propositions, which I think are
important.

1. A free act must not be thought of as a causeless act.
A causeless act is a metaphysical impossibility. The first question is therefore: what is the cause of a free act?

2. A free act must not be thought of as a motiveless act.
A motiveless act is a psychological impossibility. One might
agree to state that purposiveness is part of the phenomenologically *given* in the human act.

3. It is probably trite to take up again the proposition
that "the strongest motive always prevails". For if one asks:
what was the strongest motive in any given set of circumstances? the answer must be: "it was the one which prevailed", or else "it was some motive other than the one which
prevailed". If the former answer is given, it simply means
that I am saying that "the strongest motive was the strongest
motive", or that "the motive which prevailed was the motive
which prevailed", and this is clearly vicious circle reasoning.
But if I fall back on the second possibility, viz. that it was
some other motive, I am clearly assuming that the strongest
motive did not prevail. How then can I possibly know that
it was the strongest? The simple fact is that the notions of
strength and weakness do not apply to motives nor do they
apply to the will. We are constantly talking in metaphor
(as in this case) and then we slip into the error of thinking
that our metaphor is literally true.

4. A free act is not an unintelligible act. It is often assumed that if an act can be shown to be intelligible, that
it is thus shown not to be free. The opposite is in fact the
case. If an act is free it is free by reason of its relation to

reason. If an act is (literally) unintelligible, it will be so because it is irrational, and the irrational is not free. (Semantic note: a free act might be unreasonable, but this is a different category of assessment. It cannot be irrational, in the sense of "not related to reason".)

5. A free act in a human context is an act of a human person, and a human person in *statu viae* is this living organism. A free act must not be thought of as happening in a spirit-world vacuum, but in the context of organism. It will not be an argument against freedom to show that it is a dimension of the acts of a living organism. This is precisely what it is in human affairs. Yet it is often thought that to show a human component in an act is already to have argued against its freedom.

Responsibility

Assuming that there is such a state of the psyche in relation to an act as that which is normally called "responsibility" for it, it does not follow that this state should be thought of as an all-or-nothing state. In an older teminology, one might put it this way: given that there are factors which diminish responsibility, and that there are factors which can abolish it completely, it would be a mistake to confuse these two processes. It is possible to think in terms of a scale, with shall we say 100 arbitrary units. At the top of the scale, in an angel before the fall, one might perhaps have looked for total, 100% responsibility, on the ground that he had total knowledge, no emotions or instincts to cope with, no concupiscence, libido or aggression, no appetites of the organic order, etc., so that his act was motivated solely by total knowledge and by free election. This is possibly the reason why it was so final, so unchangeable. This level of

100% angelic responsibility is never ours. But granted that angelic status in this respect is never ours, what of the human condition? We are concerned with human acts, not angelic ones. (It is certainly a temptation in this area as in so many other areas to fall into the hazard of angelicism). Somewhere lower down on our scale is the point of highest human responsibility. This will necessarily lie well below the 100% of the angel. (Was not our intellect clouded and our will "weakened" by the fall? in addition to the fact that we are living organisms and not pure spirit anyway.) But it can still be very high on the scale. Suppose 100% responsibility for human beings lies down around the 75% level on our absolute scale. This will be a new ceiling to work towards. It will represent the position of a person who has achieved all possible human knowledge, has had the most perfect formation, the most desirable socio-economic background, has lived the life of grace all his life, has brought all the emotions and drives under control, etc. Should such a person now carry out a deliberate act, he may have 100% responsibility in human units, though still only perhaps 75% in angelic units. This is figurative, though not as fanciful as it seems, for I have perhaps just been describing Adam's situation. How far below this level of total responsibility can a man fall and still be held gravely responsible? It is sometimes thought that any drop down the scale from this ceiling of maximal responsibility automatically removes grave responsibility. This is not so. In fact, responsibility remains grave well down the scale. Thus, the fact that an act arises from, or is associated with, or affected by, an impulse, a desire, an emotion, an organic state, etc., or by socio-economic, familial or educational factors, may reduce the level from maximal possible responsibility (our figurative 100), but may still leave the act well above the threshold for grave responsibility. In fact one must go further, and state that our normal, ordinary usual human conduct is the ego-processing of behavior. To show that a behavior element enters into our conduct (e.g., to show a correlation between hormonal activity and sexual behavior) does not necessarily eliminate grave responsibility at all. Grave responsibility in human beings, like freedom, is a dimension of precisely such conduct.

Guilt

There is not just one concept or state of guilt. I propose that we distinguish the following kinds of guilt: theological, rational, normal or healthy emotional, and neurotic. Theological guilt is the state of an individual who judges that he did something wrong knowing that it was wrong, and that he was choosing to do it, and that his doing it was a violation of Divine Law. Rational guilt on the other hand is the state of a person who consciously, voluntarily and knowingly violates the natural law. These two states of course can and often do co-exist and coalesce. They are not additional specific states of awareness. They are the conditions of a human person whose judgments are as outlined. They are the concomitants of the willed act in the circumstances described. It is a mistake to think of either theological or rational guilt as consisting in some further experienced state other than the condition of the judgment of intellect in respect of the act. But this condition of theological or rational guilt ("real" guilt) will frequently co-exist with or be accompanied by the third type: normal or healthy emotional guilt. This is not a judgment, but an affective state. It is not a necessary accompaniment of the intellectual judgment, but is an indicator of the human condition. Thus an angel will not experience this kind of guilt, because an angel cannot experience emotion of any kind. Only the psycho-physical composite can experience this kind of guilt, which is rooted in infantile experience, in the anxiety provoked by the aggression of the Id, and by superego factors. The superego factors are of course acquired dimensions of emotional guilt, but the Id factors are not. Thus the "shame" of Adam cannot be attributed to superego factors since there was no one to give him a superego. They are primitive Id factors of emotional guilt deriving from anxiety produced by the release of aggression. This is the stage of healthy or normal emotional guilt. It is certainly not unhealthy for an adolescent to feel something of this emotional process. It is associated with many dimensions of behavior, particularly with the sexual. But it would be a mistake to link it too exclusively with the sexual. A normal adolescent will experience this emotional state in some form in connection with many other forms of misdemeanor. Not to experience this state at all, or not to be able to experience it, can be just as pathological as the state of neurotic guilt.

Neurotic Guilt

Neurotic guilt is a state of the emotions which may or may not accompany theological or rational guilt. It is a pathological state in much the same kay as any unhealthy prolonged indulgence of an inappropriate emotion may be unhealthy. It is further complicated by the fact that the individual who experiences it may cling to it for the masochistic pleasure of self-torture. Within neurotic guilt one may distinguish many components: fear, anxiety, dread of and desire for punishment, self-loathing, self-directed aggression, conflict between desire and aversion, etc. Neurotic guilt is allied to, but identical with, scrupulosity, and admits of many degrees. Its most usual manifestation is in connection with sexual offenses, real or imaginary. It is found in depression, hysterical states, anxiety states, schizophrenia, and involuntary states, as well as being typical of the breakthrough of the pre-moral conscience in adolescence. The pre-moral conscience includes the set of acquired behavior controls which are usually referred to as the superego (though they probably embrace a good deal more than the connotation of this term) and which operates in non-moral categories. The categories in which these controls operate are usually acceptability—unacceptability, reward-producing punishment-producing, etc., but not morally-good or morally-bad, because they are operating at a point of chronological development before that at which conscience proper (intellect judging in the context of human acts) begins to operate. But their effect is somewhat similar or analogous to that of conscience, which is why it can be called the pre-moral conscience. The sanctions of the pre-moral conscience are in the affective spheres; anxiety and dread are probably its most affective sanctions. Out of this phase grows the tabu-mechanism. Thus violation of tabu (which is non-rational and releases the powerful anxiety factors which are the pre-moral conscience's chief sanctions) generates neurotic guilt. This is why the clearest example of neurotic guilt are to be found in the conditions of compulsive-obsessional neurosis, and this was the reason also why Freud could identify the expiatory rituals of the neurotic with religion: the only guilt he acknowledged (at least verbally) was neurotic guilt, and by committing the fallacy of psycho-mechanistic parallelism, he was able to identify the guilt of the neurotic with all guilt, and the practices of the neurotic with religion.

Causation in Human Conduct

The problem of causation in respect of human conduct is complicated by the fact that we tend to confuse cause and condition. A cause is a factor which contributes positively, actively, to bringing a phenomenon about. A condition is a factor which does not contribute positively to bringing the effect about, but which enables the cause or causes to bring it about. Thus social isolation is a condition in which the suicide rate increases. But social isolation itself is not a cause, in a philosophical or scientific sense, since it describes the absence of something—a negation, or privation. It is descriptive of a condition in which certain determining co-ordinates of normal human living are missing. In a similar way a broken home, a neighborhood at the bottom of the socio-economic scale, membership of a street-gang, indeed social factors generally, operate as conditions in which certain kinds of acts occur, although most people have tended to think of them as the causes of these events. The difference beween the behavior of individuals in these circumstances, and the behavior of more privileged people is not that the less privileged behave as they do because they are determined by the presence of positive factors in their environment to behave the way they do, while the more privileged are not so determined. Paradoxically, it is the other way round. We are safeguarded, prevented from behaving in many ways which are still physically possible to us, but which in a sense have become "psychologically impossible" to us, by the presence within us of determining factors which are absent from personalities in more depressed circumstances. We need a sort of Copernican revolution in our thinking about these matters.

The factors present in us which are not present in the

delinquent, the suicide, or the psychopath, for example, can be listed as follows:

(a) knowledge—of many kinds: of right and wrong, of moral principle, of social and personal relationships, of the morals of the larger society, of law, history, geography, politics, and a host of other factors;
(b) affective attitudes, or the set of feelings (revulsion, reverence, reverential fear, self-esteem, loyalty, etc. which already establish and guarantee certain lines of conduct);
(c) unconscious control.

Within the psyche of each one of us there remains, in a dynamic or active way, a great deal of knowledge, all of it the result of learning, none of it innate, much of it in terms of pre-moral categories of evaluation (acceptability—unacceptability, affection-winning or affection-losing, approved—disapproved, rewarded—punished, for example), and almost all of it charged with pretty high-powered, primitive or infantile affective attitudes.

This emotionally-charged knowledge operates as a highly complex system of unconscious controls, and of course may in addition operate at the conscious level. Thus there are many acts of which we are physically capable, but which it is quite certain we shall never commit, not because we go through a conscious process of consideration, moral evaluation, and rejection (though we could do so, and sometimes do so as an intellectual experience) but rather because the rejection has occurred before the conception of the act as a positive possibility has ever reached consciousness. It is we paradoxically who are determined, by the process of internalization of sanctions (though it is not of course an accurate statement to say without qualification "we are determined"). More accurately, we should say that the internalization of sanctions at a pre-rational (or sub-rational) level, frees the intellect and will from some of the pressures (determining tendencies, or factors of instinct, emotion, concupiscence, libido, etc.) of the non-rational processes within us, thus liberating us, increasing our freedom, though narrowing the range of our behavior within certain dimensions (our freedom is increased in all that is most specifically and appropriately human conduct, while within the dimension of possible physical actions, e.g., violence, destructive aggressive behavior, sexual perversion, murder, etc., the range of those remaining psychologically possible is narrowed). This may sound strange. It is worthwhile therefore considering whether here and now it is possible for one to behave like a Dukhobor, or like an attendant at Dachau or Belsen, or like a teen-age gang member in a slum district—or indeed, in countless other ways. The "preventing grace" of the theologian has its natural counterpart in the set of affective factors which operate to safeguad us from carrying out many acts of which we remain physically capable.

There are two functions involved here: the superego, and the pre-moral conscience. Neither of these is conscience proper, and neither of them can be reduced wholly to the other. The superego is a set of affective dimensions of behavior which is acquired in the first eighteen months or two years of the infant's life, very largely on the basis of the attitudes conveyed to the child by its mother in inculcating ways of controlling its own instinctual movements (homeostatic processes: rhythms of sleep and waking, hunger and satiation, excretion etc.). The superego represents the first phase of control of behavior by evaluation, or by acquired checks and balances. But it operates unconsciously for the most part. Clearly it underlies the function referred to above as the pre-moral conscience, and contributes a great deal to it.

The Pre-Moral Conscience

It is important to remember that conscience in the strict sense refers to a function of intellect. It is the name of the function of intellect when intellect operates in the context of human conduct. It is sometimes said, by way of objection, that conceptions of intellect and will have tended to dominate considerations of the moral judgment. This is like objecting to the play called Hamlet because the prince of Denmark dominates the action. It is only in reference to intellect and will that the concept of moral judgment can arise. But the moral judgment can be affected by pre-moral (subrational) factors. The notion of the pre-moral conscience refers to the operation by the child from 2 to 4 or 5, of a method of conscious evaluation of acts in terms of their relation to significant persons in the child's world (mother, father, mother-surrogate, etc.). The child uses certain categories of evaluation of its behavior which may look like moral categorization in terms of (the morally) good and bad, but which in fact operate much more in terms of such dualities as acceptance—rejection, reward—punishment, and success or failure as a means to an end. It should be stressed that these, and similar categories are consciously applied by the child. They will of course be colored by the affective dimensions of the superego acting unconsciously, just as they themselves plus superego factors remain with us and affect the functioning of conscience proper.

The reductionist tendency, common to many sciences, seeks to discover, or even to impose, unity and simplicity, instead of complexity. This is in general of course a very desirable principle, referred to variously as Occam's Razor, or the Principle of Parsimony of Lloyd Morgan. But psychology is the supreme example of a science where the principle does not hold. In terms of the principle, it has been customary to "reduce" intellectual functions to sensory ones (Hume), or voluntary ones to emotional ones (Freud), or in general to reduce "higher" level functions to "lower" level ones. This has been particularly disastrous in respect of conscience, which has been "reduced" to the operation of the (unconscious) superego by so many writers that this is now often tacitly assumed to be a valid account of the matter. The important point I wish to stress here, however, is that so far from reducing two functions to one (conscience to the superego), we are constrained by the evidence to expand from two to three functions. This should not be surprising. Given a three-fold type of functioning within the psyche (rational, sensory, and unconscious, which may interlock in many ways) it will not be surprising to find evaluation of behavior occurring at all three levels. The unconscious evaluation will be in terms of the carry-over of infantile acquired attitudes from toilet-training, primitive pleasure-pain principle, etc., or in other words the superego in classical terms. But the conscious sensory evaluation of behavior is qualitatively different from this—even though the end-result may be the same. There is no conscious direction of behavior when it is superego-controlled, while it is certainly empirically the case that sensory evaluations in terms of perception, appetite, anticipation of reward and punishment, involve a conscious direction, even though it may fall far short of rational choice.

It is this conscious sensory evaluation and direction of behavior which I refer to by the term "pre-moral conscience" rather than the superego itself. Clearly the superego will have important effects on the functioning of this sensory evaluation. But precisely because it is a conscious sensory evaluation, it is not the superego itself.

We are familiar with the concept of final causality in respect of human conduct. This term refers to the notion of motivation as end, or purpose, or goal. This of course is a most important dimension of causation. But it is not the only or the whole cause of a human act. We must add to it the other three kinds of cause. Intellect supplies the formal cause, will the material cause. But the human act can also be motivated by the operation of other processes of the psyche which act as efficient causes. Thus the impulsion experienced within the psyche arising from appetite or desire is such that it exercises a form of efficient causality on the person. Similarly, the presence of imagery, throwing the organism into what used to be called a motor-set, or the operation of the presence of emotion, exciting an instinct and producing reflex organic processes are examples of the operation of efficient causality in respect of behavior.

In the mentally ill, for example in the compulsive-obsessional, the operation of efficient causality of this kind is seen very clearly. Thus the compulsive-obsessional will say that he does not wish, does not intend, to wash his hands again, and even while saying so, will actually start moving towards the wash-basin, and in spite of himself, wash his hands. Something of this kind is experienced by most people, though in a much lower degree. Responsibility is removed only when the psychical cause operates to produce behavior without the intervention of consciousness either helping it or actively condoning it. The mere occurrence of a psychical (more accurately, a psycho-physical) event which tends to produce behavior is not itself behavior, and therefore *a fortiori* is not conduct, in the sense defined. But far more important is the fact that we could not behave at all except as psycho-physical organisms. It is not a diminution of human freedom to point to the occurrence of psycho-physical processes which tend to become or function as efficient causes of human behavior. This is the precise dimension of human freedom.

8 brainwashing: has the human personality been breached?

It is commonly believed that during the last two or three decades methods have been discovered or developed whereby the thought processes, attitudes, beliefs, loyalties and aspirations of human beings (and consequently, their overt behavior) can be manipulated or altered by the use of refined techniques deriving from advances in psychology, psychiatry, pharmacology, hypnosis, applied neurology, and perhaps other specialties as well.

The popular belief about such matters is perhaps best put in the words of Edward Hunter: "Submission of body and soul, in its medieval form of confession is obligatory. The objective is to perpetrate the greatest fraud of all, by putting the victim through a conversion stage quite similar to a religious experience, but replacing his spiritual faith by a political one. These pressures give the impression of delving into trance states and witchcraft while simultaneously exploiting the latest developments in the sciences, especially in chemistry and psychiatry. The impression is correct, for this is exactly what the brainwashing treatment does. It is atavistic—a throw back—using modern tools." (*Black Book on Red China*, p. 125.)

It is possible that the popular view found its clearest

expression through Hunter, and possible also that he in turn was one of the chief molders of the popular view itself, by a sort of reciprocal causality. There are however other specifiable factors which molded the popular view. Among these one can list the following: (1) the history of the great purge trials in Moscow during 1936-37-38; (2) the trials in Hungary and elsewhere after the war; (3) the publication of George Orwell's work *Nineteen Eighty-Four;* (4) the discovery of new drugs, e.g. mescaline, and their exploitation in works of fiction, literary works, newspapers, etc., by leading writers like Aldous Huxley; (5) the experience of what happened to prisoners of war in Korea; (6) the history of Cardinal Mindszenty, especially his photographs during the trial, and his retractation-in-advance, who therefore knew or guessed what was likely to happen to him; (7) the Chinese People's Republic's institution of thought reform through the Revolutionary Colleges; and finally for this stage of the enquiry, (8) the publication of Sargant's *Battle for the Mind,* a work, which for all its disclaimers in the preface, has had the effect of producing in people's minds an attitude of irrational fear of these phenomena and the belief that the human personality has at least been breached in its innermost fortress: the assent of the will.

Probably people have always been ready to accept the myth of the evil scientist, or the mad scientist, deliberately producing a Frankenstein or unwittingly producing a Pygmalion. The myth of the alchemist dies slowly, together with the myths of witchcraft and magic. Was not Pope Sylvester II (d. 1003 A.D.) considered to be a magician because of his knowledge of and interest in mathematics? Such ideas linger perhaps unconsciously in the minds of those who assent to ideas of the "total annihilation of the human will" (Biderman and Zimmer: *The Manipulation of Human Behavior,* p. 5), and to the idea of the reduction of human beings to mere automata. Such ideas are found underlying the superstition that with the further growth of automation "we may become slaves of the machine", or the idea that with the growth of unity in Europe "we may lose our national identity". Such phrases are either a mere free-wheeling use of language to fill a gap, or else represent the emergence of primitive fears in modern dress. Other forms of these myths are found in the belief that the great electronic computers "can think", and the Vance Packard idea that we are all being manipulated by "hidden persuaders". Subliminal sensations are popular survivals of magical thinking in our midst.

There is no doubt that the attitudes of people generally to such phenomena resemble their attitudes to witchcraft and demonology (cf. the "trance states and witchcraft" of Hunter quoted above). There seems to be little doubt that we all contribute in some way to the perpetuation of these attitudes, whether by the comparatively innocuous method of mere assent to a possibility or by the more destructive method of actually asserting as fact things which are demonstrably false. An example is found in the popular presentation of hypnotism and alleged extra-sensory perception in newspapers, radio, television, etc.

There have been great developments in recent years in the treatment of mental illness by pharmacological means. It is not necessary to recapitulate these developments in detail, but only to remind ourselves of the effects of such drugs as chlorpromazine, serpasil, benzedrine, etc., which, together with all the other tools now available to psychiatry, have brought relief to many thousands who would otherwise be chronic patients in hospitals, and then to look quickly into ourselves and discover in our innermost unacknowledged thinking, clear enough survivals of a more primitive attitude to such illnesses.

It was perhaps unfortunate that these great advances in theory coincided with the exploitation of mescaline and lysergic acid by gifted journalists, and that this exploitation in turn coincided with some of the more spectacular trials. It was perhaps inevitable that all three sets of phenomena would be related to each other by many people. "Control" of the mind, "control" of the personality, "manipulation" of behavior, and many similar phrases are now commonplace language, and indeed have been accepted as possibilities by many who should have known better from their philosophical and theological training.

It is imperative to ask a number of questions, even though we may not yet be in a position to answer them all with finality. If we do not ask these questions seriously, we will fall into the trap of thinking that they do not need to be asked because we already know the answers: this was the tragedy of many with regard to witchcraft in late medieval times. See for example Sprenger and Kramer's *Malleus Maleficarum*, 1490, for a clear example of a work written simply because the elementary question: "Are there witches?" was not asked. It could not perhaps have been asked by these authors but its answer was assumed to be "yes".

The questions we must ask are:

Can a man be made to change his beliefs?
If a change occurs, how long will it last?
How are these confessions obtained?
Do those who "confess" believe their own confessions?
How successful is thought reform?

Is there any defense against it?
Have any new and hitherto obscure techniques been
discovered?
Are the processes involved really comparable to conversion?

The term brainwashing, now perhaps universal, does
not occur in the Shorter Oxford Dictionary (though the term
brainsick does) even as late as the 1959 corrected version.
This may seem surprising to some, who may have forgotten
that the very word itself was invented by Hunter, referred
to above. He translated the Chinese words *hsi-nao* in this
way, after conversations with some who had been subjected
to the program of "thought-reform" initiated by Mao-Tse-
Tung through the Revolutionary Colleges (about which,
more detailed discussion below). The lengthier term em-
ployed apparently was *szu-hsiang-kai-tsao*, meaning "ideological remolding", "ideological reform", "thought reform",
or "thought-cleansing". The transition from "thought-cleansing" through "mind-purge" to "brainwash" was perhaps
only too easy. As used by Hunter, the term was intended to
describe "an elaborate ritual of systematic indoctrination,
conversion, and self-accusation". According to Hunter, the
"elements are hunger, fatigue, tension, threats, violence, and
on occasion even drugs and hypnotism" (p. 127) combined
with "the findings of the physiologist Ivan P. Pavlov in his
experiments with dogs and monkeys to determine how reflexes can be controlled" (p. 125). The reference to Pavlov
is very common, particularly by Sargant (*op. cit.*), who
indeed would have us believe that the conditioning of reflexes is perhaps the basis of the whole process. The process
apparently led to a curious but very common form of confession—a false confession, as far as one can see—as a prelude

to conversion and eventual collaboration with the regime. The method used in China appears to have been well organized and highly stereotyped. (Lifton gives a good account of it in *Group for the Advancement of Psychiatry*, Symposium No. 4 "Methods of Forceful Indoctrination", 1790 Broadway, N. Y.: 1957)

The newcomer to the Revolutionary College was at first received into a gay, social, cheerful atmosphere. After about two weeks he began to experience the tightening-up of the regime, by means of "milieu control", or rather "total control of the milieu". This was brought about without any elaborate paraphernalia but simply by the fact that everybody was apparently expected to watch and report on everybody else, thus generating a generalized anxiety. There followed a gradual growth of uneasiness, self-accusation, and final identification with the regime. The success of this program in China may be linked with the fact that her culture is traditionally a "shame-culture" rather than a "guilt-culture". The child's behavior, and his learning of new patterns of behavior, are controlled by making him feel predominantly shame, rather than guilt. The dimension of guilt for wrongdoing is the responsibility of the parent. Thus, although an individual may not have done anything wrong, in a Western sense, he could nevertheless feel agonizing shame in its regard, and blame his parents both for the wrong-doing, and for the fact that he had done it himself not knowing it was wrong. He could thus be made to feel "guilty", i.e., thoroughly ashamed of all his previous beliefs, attitudes, loyalties, etc.: in fact of his whole culture-pattern. It would seem that this phenomenon was exploited deliberately by the Chinese Communist Government as a method of totally changing the culture. It will readily be seen that a cultural change in China from a traditional Taoist or Confucian way of life to a "westernized" type of industrial culture would be even more drastic than a change from rural peasant life in Russia to a similar type of industrial culture. Not only did Marx envisage a new human nature, but also a new culture which would produce a new nature, and which would in turn be produced by it. Soviet psychology is apparently motivated precisely by these ideas. It studies "the teaching of Marx and Engels, and Lenin; it uses dialectical materialism as its foundation; it practices criticism and self-criticism; it fights against bourgeois survivals and for the proletariat; it is a true science and on its way towards fulfilling Makarenko's motto: 'Man must be changed'". This is quoted from Hans Hiebsch's introduction to *Soviet Psychology*, a symposium contributed to by some leading contemporary Soviet psychologists (ed. Winn, Vision Press, London: 1962). Thus thought-reform in China can fairly easily be understood to mean at one and the same time the production of intense feelings of shame at having been thinking the "wrong thoughts" for most of one's life (even though one's thinking them was not one's own responsibility, but the responsibility of one's education) and the learning of a new way of thinking, i.e. the Mao way of thinking.

The application of "thought-reform" to prisoners of war in Korea was perhaps a logical development from the behavior to which the Chinese guards had themselves been subjected under the Communist regime in China. But the processes involved soon came to have overtones of magic and witchcraft, in Western eyes, and to be interpreted in terms of new scientific developments, and their application to human behavior. Thus J. A. Meerloo, (*Mental Seduction and Menticide*, Jonathan Cape: 1956) once psychology professor in Holland, and now in New York, coined the word "menticide", on the analogy of the U.N's word "genocide", to describe the process of brainwashing. Meerloo gave expression to a concept common to many who write about these matters when he said: "If the prisoner's mind proves too resistant, narcotics are given to confuse it: mescaline, marijuana, morphine, barbiturates, alcohol" (p. 30). This statement is commonly believed, but it may very well stem not from the practice of "brainwashing", but from the experience of psychotherapists who find that administering a dose of pentothal loosens a patient's tongue and facilitates the process of psychotherapy. Meerloo says later: "Modern brainwashers have tried all kinds of drugs to arrive at their devious objectives" (p. 60). He also, together with Hunter and Sargant, speaks of the use of "conditioning". This term, however, has passed into popular speech so that it is becoming more and more difficult to give it any precise meaning. Usually, in this context however, as with Meerloo, it is used to suggest that the brainwashing technique is an application of Pavlovian theory to human behavior: the production of pre-selected verbal responses by what Meerloo calls "mass-conditioning through speech". Hunter also refers to this mass process. "The effect on an entire population of a concentrated program of brainwashing would inevitably create a national neurosis" (p. 130).

In an editorial in *The Commonweal*, May 15, 1953, there is a description of brainwashing which is worth quoting because it aptly sums up the attitudes of many: "Even as a word 'brainwashing' is misjoined and ugly, and as a fact it is terrifying. But it is the monsterchild of totalitarianism, and as such comprehensible and a warning. The human personality, the totalitarians have taught us, can be breached. A man who is exhausted and hungry, who is subjected to extreme discomfort, and then questioned, argued with, patiently and skillfully, can without overt torture be brought *to say and even believe things he had once known to be false.*"

(The italics are ours.) The quotation goes on: "Many Americans who were prisoners of the Communists were subjected to this treatment." These were "the brainwashed". Biderman and Zimmer in their work *The Manipulation of Human Behavior* point out the parallel in current usage between "the brainwashed" and "the possessed". It is worth noting that the Chinese Communist authorities apparently "regard the term (brainwashing) as a quite apt and honorable description of what they wish to achieve". Biderman and Zimmer, (*op. cit.*), go on to ask "Can man really be made to behave contrary to his profoundest beliefs and his conscious self-interest?" (p. 6).

We shall now examine seriatim some of the suggestions that have been made to account for the process, and for its success.

Can the behavior of human beings be controlled by the electrical stimulation of selected areas of the cortex, as was imagined by Orwell in his *Nineteen Eighty-four?* The answer is "no". It is certainly true that in experiments on rats, direct stimulation by implanting electrodes in selected areas of the brain has produced gross changes in eating, emotional excitement, etc., and that such changes are in principle possible in the human being. In this connection, the experiments of Penfield in electrical stimulation of the cortex with a view to producing "memories" are often appealed to. It is true that Penfield has written speculatively about memory on the basis of his work, but he has also written, and many who quote him on memory fail to quote the following far more important words: "Science provides no method of controlling the mind. Scientific work on the brain does not explain the mind—not yet. Neither the work of Pavlov on conditional reflexes, nor that of any other worker, has proven the thesis of materialism. Surgeons can remove areas of the brain, physicians can destroy or deaden it with drugs and produce unpredictable fantasies, but they cannot force it to do their bidding." (Conference. Scientific Information Bureau. Vol. 2, No. 4, p. 6: 1961.) It is worth noting that nobody yet knows nearly enough about neuro-anatomy, neuro-physiology, and localization of function to use any such process in "brainwashing".

Can the behavior of human beings be controlled by the administration of drugs? Gottschalk has done a very thorough survey of the use of drugs in interrogation, published in Biderman and Zimmer, (*op. cit.*). From his survey it is clear "that drugs can operate as positive catalysts to productive interrogation" (p. 133). It may be helpful to remind the reader of some of the facts about the leading drugs before proceeding. Methamphetamine hydrochloride is known to be useful in the interrogation of the psychopath who feigns amnesia. It has been claimed indeed "that the psychopath is powerless under the influence of methamphetamine" (Brussel et al., quoted by Biderman and Zimmer), though this claim should be treated with caution. Amphetamine (benzedrine) produces a flood of ideas, emotions and memories. It used to be said that the Germans used mescaline, or some similar psychotomimetic drug, during the interrogation of prisoners of war in Europe. The psychotomimetic drugs are known to produce perceptual distortions and hallucinations, and to lead to curious euphoric or ecstatic states (see Huxley). Lysergic acid, usually referred to as LSD, is said to impair the functioning of intellect, and to distort perception, while apparently producing a strange sense of inward illumination. So far from terror, or breakdown of the personality, the experience from within seems to be one almost of "mystical" illumination and self-knowledge. The phenothiazine derivatives (e.g. chlorpromazine) have the effect of quieting or abolishing severe agitation, and reducing anxiety. This effect would seem to indicate that this drug at least would not help the interrogator, since it would in effect strengthen the hand of the prisoner. There is no report of its use in interrogation, nor of the use of serpasil or reserpine. The barbiturates can produce a lowering of attention to stimuli, a warmer and more appropriate mood, decreased anxiety, and an increased desire to enter into interpersonal relations. Thus these drugs can be of use to the interrogator. Gottschalk, to whom I am heavily in debt for the above, concludes "A person's resistance to communicating withheld information can be broken down with drugs, and particularly sodium amytal". But it is worth noting that in his investigations Lifton (*Thought Reform*) did not in fact find that the brainwashed people he interviewed had had drugs administered to them. We can conclude this section by saying that while it is true, as Gottschalk says, that drugs can facilitate communication it is not true that they can be used for purposes of "thought control" for the following reasons.

1. Too little is known about "the action of drugs on the brain in terms of both psychological and neuro-physiological mechanisms of action" to enable anyone to control the thought-processes of anybody else. ("Drugs and Brain Structure": Killam. Conference: 1962.)

2. Most experiments which have made the right distinctions and have been carried out with proper controls, give no encouragement to the suggestion of specific effects of drugs on learning processes. This means that there is no known way in which for example a prisoner can be taught under the influence of drugs to repeat verbatim and successfully a lesson in a new ideology.

3. It has been claimed by Huxley and others that the hal-

lucinogenic drugs, LSD, mescaline, etc., "open up areas of the mind not normally available to most people" with the further suggestion that these drugs may "colonize" new areas of the brain. This kind of speculation should be characterized as science fiction. The psychotomimetic drugs "can only modify or distort previously acquired information, rather than create new information". (Conference. S.I.B.: 1961.)

Can the behavior of human beings be controlled in the desired way by hypnosis? This, too, has been claimed very often. It is a regression to the schoolboy fantasy of the mysterious east of Fu-man-chu and perhaps even of Rasputin, when we assent to the use of hypnosis as a solution to the problem of brainwashing. The result of hypnosis is a lowering of the sensory threshold, and a heightening of suggestibility. Post-hypnotic suggestion can sometimes be effective. But the essence of hypnosis is dissociation: an individual can be aided to recall repressed material, and to behave temporarily in terms of dissociated areas of the personality. So far as can be ascertained, it cannot be used to teach new cognitive content. This is precisely because it deals with the lower functions: senses and emotions, and not with intellect and will. It has often been asked whether or not a hypnotized person can be "made to behave in flat contradiction with his consciously accepted moral code". Experiments in this area are few and inconclusive, but it would seem safe to answer that an individual can be induced to behave in this way if he is not in a very deep trance, provided he is conscious enough to want to do so. But if either he is conscious enough and does not want to do so, or he is in such deep trance that he could not assent to doing so, it would appear that he cannot be so induced. At least, to be a little more cautious, there is no evidence whatever that he can be so induced. Moreover, the hypnotist can have no guarantee that his process will succeed, or will last, he cannot really "control" the subject, but only make suggestions, and as far as one knows, there has never been a genuine case of a "conversion" in the sense required which could be attributed to hypnosis.

With regard to hypnosis generally, it should be pointed out that its alleged use in popular entertainment has lent credence to the possibility of a "mass hypnosis". But close examination of popular stage-shows in which hypnotism is thought to be used will show that the process is (a) not hypnosis, but (b) a clever playing on the exibitionist streak which is latent in many. The genius of the "hypnotist" or showman in these cases depends on his ability to recognize quickly the hysterics and the exibitionists among those who volunteer to come to the stage; so that others are turned away who might not be so amenable to his wishes.

Moreover it should be noted that the hypnotist depends to a very large extent on two other factors: first, the assent of the client to the possibility of his being hypnotized. Though this does not exclude the possibility of a person's being hypnotized "against his will". Assent to the possibility is quite compatible with the refusal of the will to submit, while the phrase "against his will" may only refer to the natural reluctance anyone might feel about submitting. Secondly, successful hypnosis depends far more than most people realize, on the use of "aids": thus, the suggestion "your arm is now getting warm, warmer, uncomfortably hot, etc." may be accompanied by the switching on of a concealed diathermy machine.* We may conclude (a) hypnosis

---

* "The Potential Uses of Hypnosis in Interrogation": Martin Orne. In Biderman and Zimmer, *op. cit.*, p. 208 and passim.

is not the solution to brainwashing, and (b) mass hypnosis belongs to the realm of fiction.

If neither electrical stimulation, nor drugs, nor hypnosis is the explanation, what is left? What is left is the traditional armory of the interrogator: isolation, fatigue, sensory deprivation, loss of sleep, hunger and cold. It is noteworthy that the recent work *One Day in the Life of Ivan Denisovich* by Alexander Solzhenitsyn, which appears to be a fairly accurate account of a concentration camp, stresses precisely the experience of hunger and cold. Lifton, who studied the process through eighteen months' psychiatric interviewing of a number of people who had survived brainwashing on mainland China and found their way to Hong Kong, lists the steps in the process as follows: (1) the assault upon identity, (2) the establishment of guilt, (3) self-betrayal, (4) breaking-point, represented by fear of total annihilation, (5) a change on the part of the interrogator, who substitutes leniency for sternness, and offers the chance to repent: almost a chance of a re-birth, in Pauline terms, though Lifton does not make precisely this point; next comes (6) the experience of a compulsion to confess, and once this is submitted to, in whatsoever small degree, (7) the channeling of all the victim's guilt feelings along one channel, apparently the channel of social responsibility. Finally comes (8) the re-education of the victim, after his dishonoring, so that he can once again live with himself.

In the West, we have taken for granted the operation of an objective logic and the futility of a subjective aprioristic approach to the solution of problems of an empirical scientific nature. We therefore find it extremely difficult to take seriously the operation of the dailectic in its application to affairs. But it would well behoove us to make a special study of the serious way in which the dialectic is in fact applied.

The example of Lysenko should surely be familiar to us, as well as the difficulties of Janovskaya, even in the field of pure mathematics (Bochenski, 1961). A cursory perusal of the work *Soviet Psychology,* referred to above, will suffice to convince the reader that the dialectic is taken seriously at all levels of the science. This in a sense explains the first step outlined above: the assault upon identity. A priest prisoner, for example, is "thesis": a positive commitment to the beliefs and ideals of a Christian missioner. Lifton, *Thought Reform, A Psychiatric Study of Brainwashing in China,* p. 76: 1961, shows how cleverly the priest prisoner is confronted with his antithesis. He is questioned and admits that he kept a servant, whereas he should have been the servant of all. The subject of class is thus injected. The anti-thesis of the priest, his negative identity, as it were, the part of him that he has been warned never to become, is thrown at him. A priest's negative identity as Lifton points out, is likely to include such elements as the selfish man, the sinner, the proud man, the insincere man, and the unvigilant man. Thus it was, perhaps, that Cardinal Mindszenty's picture of himself, of his self-image, was shattered by gradual undermining. The prisoner, under such an assault upon his identity, begins to doubt the more affirmative elements. Could not St. Paul himself refer to himself as the least of all the saints? There will always be a sense in which the attack of the interrogator will contain some truth. So the captive begins to doubt the more affirmative self-image (diligent priest, considerate leader, spiritual man) which had previously constituted for himself his self-image. One should never underrate the element of truth in Communist thinking: if there were not some truth co-existing with its errors, it would not be viable. We have St. Augustine's insight into error and heresy to bear us out in this.

Lifton, to whom I am greatly indebted for much of the above, speaks in his *Thought Reform, a Psychiatric Study of Brainwashing in China,* of the "lurid mythology" of thinking in terms of the "deliberate application of Pavlov's findings on dogs" to human beings, and of the belief in "an all-powerful irresistible unfathomable and magical method of achieving total control over the mind". Brainwashing he says "is of course none of these things". But he warns us also about accepting another kind of myth: the myth that "there is no such thing". The real problem is "what kind of a thing is it?"

The official reports of both the British and American governments after the experiences in Korea give us some clues. Thus in P.O.W., a report by the Secretary of Defense's advisory committee on prisoners of war, the last sentence of the text runs (p. 63) "as in the interrogation battle, the war for the minds of men is a war of wits". This is echoed from another work, that of Beck and Godin (pseudonyms of a historian and a scientist who had been subjected to the treatment, and wrote their experiences in *Russian Purge* and *The Extraction of Confession* (Hurst and Blackett, London: 1951). In this work there is no mention of drugs, nor of Pavlovian conditioning processes. They do assert however that "the NKVD developed a technique of protracted interrogation which practically no one was able to resist". The Secretary of Defense's report likewise contains many phrases which seem to indicate the impossibility of standing up to the treatment. It is quite startling to read the "doctors and psychiatrists generally conceded that 'every man has a breaking point'". This is not to be taken to mean that the report endorsed this view. It was pointed out to the committee that "The Communist interrogators had bent such men of steel as Cardinal Mindszenty". The report appears to accept that "nearly every prisoner in Korea divulged something". It has been accepted by some doctors e.g. Dr. Bryant Wedge (*G.A.P. Report,* p. 294) that it is "almost always possible to make a man give the information desired by the interrogator". The official report appears to endorse this when it says (p. 61): "At the end of World War II the consensus of the experts was this: *It is virtually impossible for anyone to resist a determined interrogator*" (italics in the Report), and again "*Although a determined interrogator cannot be resisted, he may be evaded by the prisoner*" (italics in the Report). This is important. I am going to suggest that it is this belief, more than anything else, which by its effects in determining a point of view, or an attitude, actually makes an individual vulnerable. It is true that "every man has a breaking point?" (quoted by Dr. Miller, from *P.O.W.* report, and apparently endorsed by him in *G.A.P.* Report p. 295). Our own experience of Terence MacSwiney and others would seem to indicate that this is not true. The P.O.W. report does not in fact accept this proposition, at least in so far as it is not prepared to modify the rules for prisoners divulging information. But the *Report* is revealing for another reason. It says: "The committee made a thorough investigation of the 'brainwashing' question. In some cases this time-consuming and coercive technique was used to obtain confessions. In these cases American prisoners of war were subjected to mental and physical torture, psychiatric pressures or 'Pavlov Dogs' treatment. Most of the prisoners, however, were not subjected to brainwashing, but were given a high-powered indoctrination for propaganda purposes (p. 13).

Although mentioning the "psychiatric pressures and Pavlov dogs treatment" in this passage, it is clear from the whole document and from the evidence of others (e.g., Lifton: "I have never seen any evidence that there has been any de-

liberate conscious application of Pavlovian theory". *G.A.P.*
p. 250) that indoctrination was the main weapon as it was
with Von Paulus, the Nazi German General of Stalingrad
fame, who became a convinced Communist after his capture
(*P.O.W.* p. 63). What is meant by "psychiatric pressures"
here is not clear. It would seem to mean no more than the
total control of the environment, plus the constant playing
on the fears, anxieties, hopes and dreads of the prisoners.
No evidence is offered to substantiate the assertion of "Pavlov
Dog" treatment. Presumably this is intended to refer to the
deliberate use of the conditioning of reflexes. But psychologically, this is not even possible at adult levels, for the purposes intended: i.e., to produce constant, consistent, predictable, predetermined behavior patterns to be maintained
over long periods of time, in response to a pre-determined
stimulus introduced instead of the natural stimulus for a
reflex. Miller, in the *G.A.P. Report* (p. 295), refers to the
work of Lilly and to that of Bexton, Heron and Scott, on
sensory deprivation, and to work on psychopharmaceuticals,
and says that "these methods so far as we know have not
yet been applied, at least extensively, in brainwashing". Together with so many others writing on these subjects, he
recognizes "a potential future which may be decades off"
when these things may occur. Hinkle and Wolff on the other
hand are quite explicit that brainwashing does not depend
on drugs or science (see *G.A.P.*, p. 285, 287, 288, 289), nor
on Orwellian processes (p. 293), nor on Pavlovian theory
(p. 250), but on "the three D's: Debility, dependency and
dread". Hinkle was the coordinator of a group of some twenty
investigators officially trying to "bring together the available
information on the methods of interrogation and indoctrination that are used by Communist State police" (*G.A.P.*,
p. 285). These methods "remain police methods. They are

not dependent upon drugs, hypnotism, or any other special procedure designed by scientists. No scientist took part in their design; nor do scientists take part in their operation. I confess to you that establishing a negative conclusion of this nature is difficult. I can only tell you that we have critically reviewed all the information that we could get our hands on, and this is our conclusion" (*G.A.P.*, p. 287). The essential feature of the method is isolation and repetitive interrogation, the use of much personal history; all of this carried out in an atmosphere productive of fatigue, sleep loss, and the various forms of physiological disturbance which can be produced by hunger, cold, unusual positions and the like. "Prominent features of the reactions of the prisoner are anxiety, uncertainty and intolerable discomfort . . . this leads to mental dulling, confusion, loss of discrimination and despondency associated with an intense desire to escape from the situation; and the ultimate result of this type of pressure is a state of delirium, associated with hallucinatory and delusional experiences" (*G.A.P.*, p. 288).

What then shall we conclude? I think we can come to a number of reasonable conclusions. First, I think that many people have been bewitched by the term "brainwashing" into thinking that the human personality has been breached by new scientific discoveries or their applications This is substantially not so. Nevertheless, a considerable number of people has been processed in some way which successfully brought about in their regard behavior which would not have been foreseen. In many of these cases, the explanation is simple enough: the behavior was that of individuals "who, having finally submitted to pressures to comply, attempted to maintain a status which appeared to be consistent with survival and for which it was possible to muster up rationalizations" (*G.A.P.*, p. 284).

Thus to our first question, at the outset of this essay we can answer: Yes. A man can be made verbally to change his beliefs, but not by any new inventions, diabolical or otherwise. Rather by the oldest techniques of all: self-interest, terror, deprivation. But in so far as a genuine change of "belief" occurs, as distinct from a verbal declaration of a belief, the change will be due to some genuine element of truth in the indoctrination. To our second question (if a change occurs, how long will it last?) the answer seems to be: just so long as either self-interest, or the pressures of the environment, or both, demand it. To our third question: How are these confessions obtained? the answer will be along the lines indicated in the last paragraph or two. Those who "confess" do not believe their own confessions, in so far as these are mere conforming documents, obtained under duress. But thought reform is a different matter. In the sense intended by Mao ("The entire purpose is to save the person, not to cure him to death") thought reform achieves its consistent Communist purpose: but then may one suggest that thought reform is not what was intended by the term "brainwashing", though the latter was apparently intended as a translation of the former.

The processes involved are not really comparable to conversion, in spite of what Sargant says. Thus Lifton says: "It is quite clear that thought reform resembles, in many features, an induced religious conversion, as well as a coercive form of psychotherapy. These comparisons can be made profitably, but should not be put forth loosely. There remain important differences among these various approaches to 'changing' the individual personality" (*G.A.P.*, p. 249). Perhaps the real difference between what happens in "brainwashing" and what happens in other circumstances is describable in terms of Newman's distinction of notional and real assent. Notional assent can be given to a proposition not known to be true, but assented to on grounds other than evidence, while real assent is brought about by evidence, based on real understanding. Thus notional assent can be given to a proposition on grounds of its origin, prestige, pragmatic value, or shame producing efficacy, and perhaps in principle even on Pavlovian grounds (reiteration, etc.) but real assent can only be given if the proposition is properly understood and the evidence for it seen to be cogent, and this is clearly missing from any Pavlovian conditioning process.

Finally we must ask: how do we account for the fact that so many people could unexpectedly be found to behave in ways which flagrantly conflicted with their traditional beliefs, way of life and scale of values. May I put the answer this way: assent to the possibility of being brainwashed leaves a man in the precise position of being a potential victim of the process. For as soon as one has assented to the possibility of being breached from without, one has already been breached. In other words, if one really believes that one person can so subject another to pressures and treatment that he will behave in these ways, resistance while still theoretically possible becomes practically unavailing and impossible. The victim thinks: "I shall yield eventually. No one can really resist. Every man has his breaking point. If they are going to break me eventually, why don't I give in now? It would be better to give in now while I am still at least partially in control of myself, and of my mind, than to hold out and confess or conform when they have reduced me to an automaton. At least I can save something from the wreck now, but nothing later." Then having capitulated it is easy to rationalize the position by an assertion of brainwashing in the witchcraft sense spoken of above. "If I had in fact been brainwashed, I would not be responsible for my acts, and would therefore have to be excused, indeed even pitied, and sympathized with for my apparent treason. Therefore I was brainwashed."

There is no doubt that prisoners are subjected to inhuman pressures and torments. But the more we spread among people the idea that in spite of their best endeavors, in spite of their goodwill, courage, endurance, and the grace of God, they are nevertheless powerless in the face of a new diabolical, and scientifically efficacious threat, the more we leave them vulnerable in the face of such a threat. We aid the very process itself by leading people to assent to its possibility. We know that God, who knows our weakness, will not suffer us to be tempted beyond that which we are able to resist (St. Paul). We know moreover that while conforming behavior, overt acts, can be brought about by the use of fear and force (*vi et metu* is a hallowed phrase in Canon Law and in moral theology) the assent of the will cannot be brought about. If there should appear to be an internal assent, this will be an illusion. The human person remains invulnerable in precisely that which constitutes his human personality, his intellect and will.

Finally, let us ask, who or what kind of people can be brainwashed in this modified sense? The American evidence shows that the less well-informed were perhaps the most vulnerable. They were most easily indoctrinated. But as against this there remains the towering figure of Cardinal Mindszenty. In his case it is clear, from his retraction written in advance of his "confession", that he really assented to the possibility of being brainwashed.

I would suggest, as a tentative conclusion from the evidence to date, that the vulnerable are those who have never undergone the primordial experience of cold, hunger, thirst and sleeplessness, and who thus do not know the capacity of the organism to endure. They have never been near the biological limits, and do not know that they are almost impossible to reach. This coupled with the belief in the efficacy of the process itself, a low anxiety threshold, and an insufficient awareness of the consistent logic (though perhaps in non-logical categories) of those who believe the dialectic, leaves an individual vulnerable. Having raised a generation who have never had it so good, we may have exposed them unwittingly to evil. How many of us have ever been really hungry, thirsty, cold or sleepless?

9 the natural phenomena of mental suffering

There is a very real sense in which all pain and suffering are mental phenomena. The actual lesion of a part of the anatomy is not the pain one suffers—the cavity in the tooth is not the toothache—but it is very important not to make the mistake of some well-intentioned people of thinking that because a pain is not to be identified with the injury done to the organism, that therefore it is not real. The confusion here is that of the Christian Scientists, for instance, as also of a great many faith-healers of all kinds. The fact that a phenomenon is mental is clearly not the same as saying that it is not real. We are misled by our own modes of speech, sometimes, into grave error. To tell someone that his trouble is "all his imagination" is very often literally true, though wholly false in the sense in which the speaker uses the words. For the speaker intends to convey to his hearer that his trouble is not real, but only imaginary. The real trouble is that imaginary trouble is the most distressing, because the most real of all.

Physical courage, it has often been pointed out, is very easy. How many hundreds of thousands of ordinary men, women and children exhibited an incredible degree of physical courage during the late war in the face of air-raids and the shell-fire of advancing armies? True, there were some casualties, some whose courage failed them and whose nerve, in the popular phrase (but again how misleading it is) cracked under the strain. Before the war, when the threat of total war was imminent and the experts did not know and could not guess how great masses of population would stand up to the horrors of "blanket" bombing, it was expected that great numbers would crack under the strain. A high increase in the incidence of neuroses was expected, and emergency services were devised to deal with the expected flood of patients suffering from hysterical or anxiety conditions. But the odd thing was that so far from increasing, these forms of illness among the civilian population actually showed a decrease. Similarly, the expected increase of neurotic disorders among combat troops due to the terrifying instruments of war which were in use did not take place either. True, there were better psychiatric services available during the second world war than were ever available to combat troops before, and conditions which during the first world war, for instance, were thought to be physical or physiological, were now seen to be psychogenic, and being properly diagnosed, could now be cured. But even so, it was most impressive to note how ordinary men who would make no claim to be heroes, whose courage would fail them on the football field if tackled by an opposing giant while in possession of the ball, who would tremble at the prospect of a reprimand from their employer, nevertheless stood up without a tremor to weapons and dangers which in cold blood would strike terror into the onlooker's breast. This phenomenon is generally classed under the head of "morale" —which is best understood, I suggest, as a combination of emotional motivation and voluntary determination to achieve an end.

Physical courage is easy because physical pain is easy. Notice how it is possible, though unpleasant and extremely painful, to stand up to the dentist's drill, even when he is in contact with an exposed nerve. We all fight shy of the experience, but the odd thing is that we can all face up to it too. Or consider the physical pain which is generally regarded as the most excruciating in human experience—the pain of a "stone" moving through the kidney. Even this can be borne without unconsciousness or death. The truth of the matter is that with regard to physical pain we operate what might be called a self-regulating compensatory mechanism: as long as a physical pain can be borne, we bear it, and sometimes at least we can ignore its unpleasantness. When it cannot be borne, we cease to bear it, because we sink into unconsciousness. But perhaps the oddest thing about physical pain is that there are no pain-receptors in the brain itself.

To understand mental suffering, it is important to be clear about physical pain. Sometimes physical pain is accompanied by mental suffering: the dread of the dentist's drill is probably due to one part physical pain, and nine parts fear of physical pain. The latter is a mental phenomenon causing mental suffering. Let us call the first part "reluctance due to pain" and the other nine parts "reluctance due to fear". In general, anxiety is simply fear protracted through time. But there is an important psychological difference between the two. Fear is an emotion, usually unpleasant, which is aroused by a threat to the organism arising from some stimulus in the environment, whose purpose is to throw the organism on the defensive with a view to ensuring survival. It is unpleasant for the very good reason that if it were pleasant we might seek to protract the experience which produces it, and thus instead of ensuring survival by taking avoiding action, we might actually bring about the destruction of the organism.

That is its biological significance. Notice that below the human level, no organism seeks to experience fear. But at the human level we find a distortion of emotional life even here. For human beings have devised ways of experiencing this emotion which makes it attractive and pleasant. The terror (and it is a real terror, even though its cause may not be real) which a cinema audience experiences during a thriller or horror film is a case in point. A recent series of photographs of children at a movie shows clearly that the dominant emotion they were experiencing was fear. Yet they came and enjoyed the show. A somewhat less unhealthy example of this distortion of emotional life is to be found in the "screams of delighted terror" from people riding on a switchback railway at a fun-fair.

But anxiety is a different matter. While it is true to say, as we have just said, that in general anxiety is fear protracted through time, nevertheless there is a difference. Always, if you examine it, you will find that anxiety involves people. You may be afraid of an examination. But if you are anxious about it, and really honest with yourself, you will find that what is really worrying you is not the examination but the possible effects of your failing it on your reputation, which of course strictly involves other people. You will see this more clearly if you try to think of what your attitude would be to an examination whose results were to be for ever locked away in the breast of the examiner.

Fear and anxiety are the major disintegrating forces of human mental life. I would go further, and say that at the natural level they are the causes of nearly all mental suffering. If we add to them a condition which we can call "pain of loss at the natural level" (analogous to the "pain of loss" which is characteristic of the suffering of the damned) we shall have, I suggest, a complete picture of the causes of mental suffering.

It is superfluous to ask: how real is mental suffering? If you remember that an organism must be conscious in order to feel pain even of the physical kind, you will see that mental suffering is strictly the only kind of suffering there is. You can anaesthetize the pain-producing organ or region of the anatomy (in most cases without producing total anaesthesia). But to produce relief from mental suffering no such simple technique is available. There are, however, techniques called "defense mechanisms", of which more anon, which the organism uses to avoid or eliminate mental suffering. These are analogous to the relapse of the organism into unconsciousness under stress of great physical pain, since in essence they consist either in "selective inattention" whereby the organism does not allow itself to face the unpleasant cause, or "repression" whereby, having faced it and found it unpleasant, it succeeds, at least for a time in pushing the whole matter into the unconscious.

The number of things of which we can be afraid is legion. But at the human level there are strictly only three fears. These three fears are universal, because they belong to our finiteness, to our need for security, and to our extraordinary Matter-and-Spirit nature. The first of these is the fear of growing up. That is the name I give to our fear of the future, of the unknown, of the dark. It is manifested most particularly in adolescence, where it is seen as a reluctance to undertake the responsibilities of adulthood, and manifested usually as a clinging to the security of childhood. We need security and cry out for it at all stages of our existence. We actually achieve it only in childhood, where emotional security is provided by loving parents, and all our other needs are met insofar as parents doing their best can meet them. The fixation at an infantile level of development, and the regression to infantile modes of behavior of which analysts speak, are due directly to the fear of growing up, with consequential clinging to a stage of development where this fear did not arise. The marked appearance of this fear in adolescence is due to the sudden expansion of our capacity for emotional experience at this stage of development together with the unknown and unforeseeable events which lie in the years ahead. For most of us going through a normal adolescence this fear never reaches consciousness, or at any rate never in a very marked form. But for those to whom it appears fully formed in consciousness, it constitutes one of the great causes of mental suffering. Various ways are devised by the mind for dealing with it. One of them is the refuge of a purely fantasy world. Some elements of fantasy, of day-dreaming, are characteristic of all adolescents. But when the fantasy world is substituted for the real world, as happens sometimes, the resulting condition is called schizophrenia. This can be a most painful illness, since the patient's mind is the subject of fears from two sources: he is afraid to face the real world in any shape or form, and he is also afraid of the contents which he finds in his own mind welling up from unconscious depths.

The second of the great human fears is the fear of losing one's reason. Let me hasten to reassure the reader that the presence of this fear in the conscious mind is one of the surest guarantees against ever losing one's reason, since its presence is the surest sign of the maintenance of insight into oneself. In dreams and fantasies, in the experience of impulses and wishes (very often irrational and disguised), in the awareness of primitive aggression, one comes face to face with the non-rational side of human mental life, a phenomenon at once attractive and repulsive. The striving of the rational principle to retain control against the increasing power of sick emotions constitutes one of the most painful experiences known to man on the natural plane. For the majority this fear has rarely to be consciously faced, but if you ever meet anyone who is struggling with it in full consciousness you will really come to know the meaning of mental suffering. We are too much inclined to think that those who are mentally ill are essentially happy, that the pain of mental illness is really suffered by the relatives of the sick person. But it is worth remembering that only the patient who has finally lost all insight into his condition and is wholly out of touch with reality, and is moreover in a euphoric phase, is happy. For the rest, pain, suffering and unhappiness are the rule.

The third great fear is the fear of death. This is a universal phenomenon in living organisms. In the case of non-sentient life, it is not of course an emotional experience, since the vegetative world is incapable of sentient awareness. But notice how even at this level, no organism seeks its own destruction, but clings tenaciously to life. On its positive side this fear is best thought of as the instinct of self-preservation. But this is not quite accurate. The fear is the guarantee that this instinct will achieve its end. From the dawn of full consciousness of self this fear begins to operate. It is with us at all times, coloring and conditioning all that we do. It reaches down to the deepest regions of the psyche on the vegetative and sentient level, and stretches upwards to the highest peaks of rational life. How much the more potent will it not become for enlightened and regenerate human nature which realizes the real significance of death and what lies beyond. If any man does not fear death, it has been very well said, he is either a saint or a fool. He either has nothing to fear because he has lived perfectly and has achieved a correct scale of values, or else he has lost all insight into his real nature and has become a creature of unreason. If you pause a moment and consider all the things of which a man might be afraid, you will see that he is afraid of them not for what they are, but because they are either analogues or potential causes, or symbols, or conditions, or consequences of death. A man is afraid of airplanes? No, he is afraid of dying in an air crash. He is afraid of anaesthesia? No, he is afraid either of the operation to follow, which may be fatal, or else he is directly and primitively afraid of the anaesthetized state as an analogue of death. He is full of fears and depressions, terrified and miserable, torn between self-loathing and self-pity, in the condition described as involutional melancholia (which hits all men who live long enough!) and tells you he is afraid of hidden enemies, or of poverty, or of disastrous consequences for his wife if he goes smash? No, he is afraid of death, which with the growing awareness of failing powers, and the consciousness of time running out, has become perhaps for the first time the most real event in his world. You meet a hypochondriac, absurdly and childishly worried about insignificant pains or non-existent symptoms. You wonder how he can be such a fool. He is perfectly orientated in all other spheres, but in the sphere of his health he has become an irrational creature. Once again the explanation is simple. He is afraid of all the predisposing conditions, the symbols, of the disintegration of the organism. The deep bass notes of the fear of death carry out their own theme and color every bar of the melody of life. The child afraid in the dark, the sailor afraid to begin a journey on a Friday, the superstitious spinster afraid of spilt salt, all are afraid of death. The ritual of primitive religions, magic spells and charms, the miser's hoard and the millionaire's unnecessary bank-

balances, as well as absurd though generous gestures of phil-
anthropy and great national and international defense organizations, all spring from the same ultimate source, the fear
of death. But the human mind is clever. If the conscious
mind faced this fear in cold blood and recognized it for what
it is, it might find the experience insupportably painful.
Or it might have the effect of changing radically one's scale
of values and way of living. Hence the mind refuses to face
the fear for what it is. It successfully disguises it under one
or other of the myriad forms of which in its ingenuity it is
capable. Or it avails of one of the mechanisms of defense
to which I referred earlier. It simply represses the whole fear
lock stock and barrel into the unconscious mind. It will not
think of death in any shape or form. But of course the unconscious mind is thinking of nothing else, and the fear is
there like steam in an overheated boiler, seeking an outlet
but with no safety valve to draw off the surplus and dangerous energy. The result is what the psychologist calls conflict.

Conflict is the way in which mental suffering due to fear
manifests itself. Its forms are many, but essentially for our
purpose it is a clash between a deep-rooted impulse to action
and the restraining or repressive forces either of the unconscious mind itself, or of the conscious mind. Conflict is the
cause of very painful suffering. The child who wants to run
away from the ferocious dog, but is blocked by a gate which
he cannot open, the soldier in battle who wants to run away
but is checked by the thought that his own officer will shoot
him if he does (or more powerfully checked by the thought
of the disgrace if he does), the upsurge of sheer animal
instincts which are blocked at once from issuing in action
either by conscious control, or by unconscious forces, all
illustrate occurrence of conflict. But suppose that both the
impulse to action and the restraining forces are wholly uncon-

scious, what then? In this case the conflict as such does not reach full awareness. What emerges in the conscious mind is a diffused malaise, an inexplicable free-floating anxiety, a dull puzzled painful throbbing of incomprehensible movements of pain, depression, sorrow, fear and dread. This is the "anxiety neurosis" of which psychiatrists speak.

There is another and more familiar form of conflict, nearer to ordinary life—in fact part and parcel of ordinary life—while at the same time a more extreme form of it is found in psychopathological states. This should perhaps more correctly be called frustration—it is the blocking of an emotional movement such as is found in unrequited love. The mother whose beloved son deserts her, or whose deep maternal love is met only by coldness, contempt, ingratitude or worse suffers so that she can cry out: How sharper than a serpent's tooth it is to have a thankless child!

The existentialist writings have brought out into bold relief the all-pervading pain of anxiety in human life. The fears of which we have been speaking are the main sources of mental suffering, but there remain two further sources: the conflict between my awareness of self and my consciousness of my standing with others—picturesquely put by Sartre in the memorable words: *L'enfer, c'est les autres;* and the suffering due to the loss of a loved object, which I have called the pain of loss at the natural level.

If *per impossibile* no other person, human or divine, existed, there would be no anxiety. There would certainly be fears, but they would be fears of natural objects and calamities. But there would be no reproaches or fear of reproaches from without, no worries or anxieties about others, no emotional attachments or entanglements, no responsibilities and no reckoning. But the existence of others is an inescapable fact, as also is the existence of God, and so there is found a whole new sphere of suffering, generated by the relations in which we stand to other persons, both human and divine. With human persons all our relations are fraught with anxiety; have we not said that anxiety always involves other people? We can now say that other people always involve anxieties.

Finally, and in a sense primarily, there remains the great source of suffering due to the loss of a loved object. When the movement of love for another is blocked, the result is pain. The deeper and the more-pervading the love, the greater the pain. Why should this be so? When a mother loses a child, a child a parent, a wife a husband, or a lover his be-trothed, the emotional movement towards the loved object does not at once cease. Rather is the whole world of emo-tional life thrown into turmoil by the generation and release of other perhaps deeper and more vivid emotions: sorrow, desire, hatred (for oneself), fear of the future, while all the time the inability to do anything about it and the futility of the emotions being experienced beats inexorably on con-sciousness. The result is a great series of conflicts and frustra-tions generating a kind and degree of suffering which even the greatest poets can only inadequately express. Peace, though not always consolation, supervenes eventually be-cause the forces spend themselves sooner or later. But suffer-ing of this kind can sometimes be so great that before the forces have spent themselves, the conscious mind finds it can no longer support the intensity of grief and takes refuge in the irrational world of fantasy, much as the organism in the presence of insupportable pain takes refuge in uncon-sciousness.

We shall never eliminate fear and anxiety from human life, since we can never escape the thought of death, or live in a world devoid of other people. But we can do much to alleviate the burthen of human mental suffering, negatively or prophylactically, by not adding to it, by preparing people for it, by understanding it when we meet it; and positively or therapeutically, by availing of the twin means, natural and supernatural, of dealing with it. The supernatural means of prayer and grace, of faith hope and charity, in fact the Sermon on the Mount, are the most important. But one should not neglect the use of the means which the advances in psychology and psychiatry have placed at our disposal.

10 psychopathology and mystical phenomena

Both experimental psychology and psychopathology have made valuable contributions to our knowledge of the phenomena of visual and auditory hallucinations, while the "depth"' psychologists, by analytic studies and medical and psychiatric researches in psycho-'somatic' problems have thrown a good deal of light on the complex physiological consequences of emotional states. Some at least of this knowledge is relevant in a proper assessment of the nature and value of certain sensory and intellectual processes met with in the lives of some saintly people, and allied or similar processes met with in the lives of some who are not so saintly.

The greatest difficulty in practice in considering psychical, psychological and mystical phenomena is not, as one might suppose, the inherent difficulty of the subject-matter, but rather the purely semantic one of knowing what one is talking about. Words are used in psychological and mystical literature which seem to be the same as those of ordinary intelligent speech, but on examination it emerges that the objects they denote are very different. The word mystical illustrates the point fairly well. Too often it is used as the logical contrary of real, or clear, or literal, or a combination of these while a mystic is confused with a visionary, and a visionary in turn is taken to be one who is too aetherial to be occupied with mundane affairs, or too idealistic to seek for an attainable ideal. Most people, it would seem, confuse mystical with mythical or mysterious, while many seem to think that it has something to do with "misty", when visibility is low, and the outlook obscure. The whole problem is still further obscured by the use of mystical to describe certain poets, or certain kinds of poetry. A poet is not a mystic because his poetry is about abstract or theological concepts, nor even because it seems to derive from a supernatural interpretation of sensory experience, as in Joseph Mary Plunkett's "I see His Blood upon the Rose", but only if the content of the poems he writes is the result of an inspired experience wrought by the Holy Ghost in his intellect and will, as in St. John of the Cross. Being a visionary has nothing whatever to do with abstract painting, or El Greco landscapes, or fortune-telling, or adolescent dreams of youths with arms outstretched, silhouetted against the rising sun. Being a visionary means seeing visions, and seeing visions has a lot in common with the phenomena of illusion, hallucination and imagery. Being a mystic, on the other hand, need not include seeing visions, or being suspended in mid-air in ecstasy. Being a mystic means being a soul so purified that intellect and will are subjected to the power of the Holy Spirit, who infuses a mode of prayer, and sometimes a degree of knowledge, which the unaided human being does not achieve. This can and does take place without any extraneous and unnecessary aid of visions and "interior voices", though most mystics have perhaps had the aid of these secondary and accidental phenomena (this is the teaching of St. Teresa and St. John of the Cross) in order to lead them to mystical contemplation.

With regard to the phenomena of mysticism in its proper

sense (inspired contemplation), psychology and psychopathology have nothing positive to contribute, and for the very good reason that infused contemplation is brought about by grace, which does not destroy, but perfects and elevates the natural capacities. But in the other field, that of visions and revelations, they have an important role to play. One should be constantly alive to the possibility of mistaking hysterical or hallucinatory phenomena for visions and revelations whose source is divine, as well as to the possibility that God may use the natural phenomena of the senses and imagination to achieve his ends, so that in a given case a vision, for example, might be the same kind of phenomena as an hallucination—in other words, a very natural and almost normal event in psychopathology, but used by God, as he might use any other phenomena of the natural order, for a purpose of his own.

Father Gabriel, O.D.C. has pointed out that "even in our own day, there is too much credulity in this department, and it is a credulity that leads to deplorable consequences, which are inimical to the real progress of the spiritual life". Just before that he says: "Although the attitude of these mental scientists with respect to such extraordinary graces has become increasingly severe, nevertheless we cannot say that among spiritual persons an attitude of prudence in regard to these matters is as yet general." (*Visions and Revelations in the Spiritual Life,* Mercier Press: 1950.)

Father Gabriel does not discuss in detail the psychology and psychopathology of visions, revelations and their analogous phenomena on the natural plane. But he tells us that "we must not forget that man carries about with him all the idiosyncracies of his own nature, even into his spiritual life, and the religious coloring wherewith he paints certain morbid phenomena does not alter their worthlesness." This is salutary advice. Anyone who thinks that the Church too readily accepts phenomena such as apparitions, private revelations, or stigmata, would do well to remember that Father Gabriel reminds us of nothing new in this field, but only underlines, on the authority of the Mystical Doctor of the Church, St. John of the Cross, and the great St. Teresa, what has always been the strict ecclesiastical position. The stigmata of St. Francis of Assisi, St. Catherine of Siena, and St. Gemma Galgani are recognized authoritatively but besides these there are few, if any, others. Father Thurston, S.J. once pointed out that in Belgium alone in the nineteenth century there were two hundred alleged stigmatists, not one of whom was declared authentic by the Church. And the number of apparitions of Our Lady which have been officially sanctioned, compared with the number of claims made, gives startling statistical evidence of the caution of ecclesiastical authority in this field.

It may be of interest to state some of the facts that must be borne in mind in connection with visions and revelations. From philosophy and psychology we learn something of the normal processes of cognition of the human mind. In the interaction of organism and environment, certain nerve-endings (called the peripheral receptors) respond to their adequate and proper stimuli, physical, electro-magnetic, or chemical, as the case may be. The result of this stimulation is the process called sensation. As a cognitive process, however, this must be distinguished from the mere mechanism of stimulus and response as studied in physiology. This latter mediates sensation as a cognitive process, and must not itself be identified with sensation, as too often happens in physiological text-books. The cognitive process presupposes the intact organ, and the intact organism, while the physiological process can be studied as an isolated mechanism, or even paralleled by non-organic physical, chemical and electro-magnetic processes. In the intact conscious organism, the process of perception supervenes at once on the process of sensation. This means that instead of becoming aware of mere sensory data—colors, sounds, smells—or of the stimulation of the end receptors, we become aware instead of things—meanings, or meaningful experiences. We "see" tables, chairs, people, oranges and lemons, and not just patches of color of various dimensions. The psychology of perception is vastly complicated, both by subjective factors and processes, and by external conditions. Always, however, a synthesis of sensory data is effected, and memory and imagination play their part. Memory enables us to recall similar phenomena, and recognize the present material, while imagination supplements the present fragmentary sensory material with data from the same or other sensory modalities. Intellect, by abstraction from the sensory material, forms concepts which lead to understanding and generalization. One cannot stress too often the fact that there is no knowledge in the mind other than what has been received through the external senses, molded in perception, or abstracted by intellect. There is no other channel through which knowledge of any kind can be naturally attained. The alleged phenomena of telepathy and para-psychology generally would require an extensive treatment on their own. It is enough to say for the moment that there is no such thing as extra-sensory perception (with all due respect for the scientific integrity of J. B. Rhine and his followers). The temptation to think that somehow the mind is equipped naturally with some form of innate knowledge has constantly misled philosophers and perhaps other generally more reasonable people, from Plato through Descartes to the Archetypal images of the Universal Unconscious of Jung.

But the fact that there is no innate cognitive content in the human mind, and that all its natural knowledge is acquired through sensory experience and the subsequent normal cognitive processes, does not mean that praeternaturally or supernaturally no other kind of knowledge can be acquired. If, however, God or some other intellectual agent wishes to give a further kind of knowledge to a human being, how can it take place? Man's nature being what it is, and God's omnipotence being what it is, the only possibilities (apart from a radical change in human nature itself) are either (a) the production of the effects of a normal stimulation of the peripheral receptors without an adequate stimulus, or (b) the production of the sensory synthesis which would normally be the result of perception without adequate sensory material to work on, or (c) the direct production in the intellect of a conceptual content without the process of abstraction from sensory material. In fact all three types of knowledge are found in the lives of visionaries and mystics, and the first two are also found in morbid states of pathological personalities. Moreover, the first two, but not the third, can be produced by disembodied finite intelligences. The third since it involves intellect is immediately subject only to God. (Intellect and will being rational, and therefore the capacities which specifically render man a person, are safeguarded by the inviolability of personality. They may, however, be indirectly affected through the production of effects in sensory and perpetual processes, on which they depend extrinsically for their material. Hence the dangers for both in the phenomena of obsession and possession.)

When a cognitive content is produced in either of the first two ways, it is called in the case of (a) an external vision, and in the case of (b) an imaginary vision. The term "imaginary vision" is psychologically acceptable, but colloquially misleading. "Imaginary" is one of the words referred to at the outset as different in ordinary speech and in technical language. Here it does not mean unreal, or fictitious, or fabricated, but is simply the adjectival form of the noun imagination (which is defined as the capacity of the mind to re-instate in consciousness the product of sensory stimulation in the absence of an adequate stimulus), and it means simply "the product of imagination". An image of this kind can be infused by God, or by the devil, but its character will be such as might have been produced by a human imagination given the requisite material. An external vision, on the other hand, and regarded strictly as a phenomenon different in mode from the imaginary vision, can be of three kinds. There is nothing to prevent the omnipotence of God, or the unknown power of the devil, from stimulating a peripheral receptor, so that the effect will be such as might have been produced by an adequate stimulus. Clearly this will give an "external vision"—i.e., the cognitive experience of seeing something, with no natural cause to account for it. The second possible kind is the production of a sensory object or percept (e.g. a picture, statue, or apparition) which then stimulates the receptors in the normal way. The third kind of external vision, however, is the very commonplace phenomenon of hallucination. As Father Gabriel has pointed out, both visions of this kind and hallucinations "may be the work of the same psychological mechanism". But he adds, "the cause which sets the mechanism in motion is completely different".

In order to understand the nature of hallucination, some understanding of the normal functioning of imagery is necessary first. In ordinary language we use the word image either for an object which is designed to resemble in some way some other object; or if we are thinking of mental images, we use it almost exclusively for visual images. It is important to note at once that psychologically an image can belong to any one of the sensory modalities—visual, auditory, tactile, etc. An image in the psychological sense is any sensory representation of any kind which emerges in consciousness otherwise than by the stimulation of a peripheral receptor. Normally (in the sense of "for the most part") this kind of sensory representation will be less vivid, less intense, less complete than the immediate result of perception ("the percept"). But this need not be so. There are several kinds of image which can be just as vivid as the percept—sometimes more so. These are still "normal", in the sense that, while they may not be found "for the most part", they are certainly not abnormal phenomena. The "primary memory" image is of this kind—the image we unconsciously carry of the first few words of a sentence, while listening to the end. The image of an object in an artist's mind when, in the popular phrase, he "paints from memory", or which he bears of his model while studying his canvas even when he paints from life is of this order. But especially the "eidetic" image which is found in about 50 per cent of all children and young adolescents illustrates the point. The child so gifted can look at a complicated pattern (e.g., a picture, or a series of small objects) for a space of time too brief to allow the accurate study of even a fraction of the whole, and can then "project" the image on to a neutral ground and read off the details. For the most part this must be done quickly after the stimulation of the receptors. But the image may reappear later, at unknown intervals of time. This image is plastic, modifiable, and can assume a vividness of coloring or accurate delineation of line greater than that of the original stimulus-pattern. It can be either voluntary or involuntary. If the "ground" is moved, e.g., through an angle of 90 degrees, the child will

turn his head and "follow" the revolving image. This, however, is not hallucination. The child retains complete insight,
and knows he is not "seeing" an objective picture. In the
case of hallucination insight is the first thing to go, and the
individual really believes he is experiencing a trans-subjective percept. But the point at the moment is simply this:
the degree of vividness of an image is not the measure of its
normality.

In the ordinary operation of mind an image does not
occur as an isolated phenomenon, but as one event in a
complicated structure, in which emotion, impulse, instinct
and desire can play a part. The emotional tone and motor
set of an image are perfectly normal factors, in both senses
of normal mentioned above. The important fact, however,
is that while normally an image arouses an emotion, the
causal sequence can readily operate the other way, so that
the experience of an emotion can produce a flood of imagery.
The lover, experiencing a flood of tender emotion, sees the
loved one in every face in a crowd. This is the case also with
children, who, on experiencing loneliness or a loss of the
sense of security in the dark, proceed to experience the
emotion of fear, which at once peoples their "imagination"
(and the room) with specters and ogres. Exactly the same
phenomenon takes place in anxiety-states at adult levels
(especially the "free-floating" anxiety), and in some phases of
paranoia and schizophrenia. The process is the same in the
normal and abnormal states; only the content, and the degree of insight into the reality or trans-subjectivity of the
projected image is different.

There is no reason to expect among holy people a higher
percentage of normally balanced minds than throughout
the rest of the population. If anything, one might expect,
at any rate in some social conditions, a higher percentage of

maladjusted people leaning for support on religion. There are then two factors to be reckoned with: a person of unbalanced emotional pattern may, under the stimulus of an emotion, produce an image (in the literal sense) whose content will be that of the kind of imagery most prevalent in his mind—and in the case of a religious person given to the practice of "composition of place" in meditation, or who mistakes imagery for thinking, this will most likely be imagery of a religious character. The process of projection (as described above) can then bring about hallucination. The other possibility is that children and young adolescents whose eidetic imagery is particularly vivid, may project on to a neutral background (e.g., a dark recess, or a cloud) an eidetic image corresponding to a statue or picture they have seen. It is worth noting that the so-called phenomenon of "photographic memory" is nothing but a carry-over of the gift of eidetic imagery into adulthood. It is not to be wondered at, therefore, that some adults will produce hallucinations of this type. For the sake of clarity, it must be stated that the word hallucination is used here because an eidetic image in which insight into its subjective character is lacking conforms fully to the psychology of hallucination. Moreover, hallucination does not necessarily mean a morbid state of mental health, any more than illusion does.

With regard to private revelations, much the same considerations must be borne in mind. By private revelations we mean the phenomena experienced by mystics, visionaries and others, of hearing voices. The voice may be heard as a third party speaking in the ordinary trans-subjective way, or it may be heard "within". St. Teresa mentions a third kind of voice, in which the words are planted in the very center of the soul, in their full meaning and authoritatively. This last seems to be part of the phenomenon of direct divine illumination of the intellect and is not under consideration here. The first two, however, must be considered. The first may be the production, by divine or diabolic power, of the normal physical stimulus for hearing—vibrations of an elastic medium. Or it may be the direct excitation of the basilar membrane by the same sources. The voice heard "within" however, may be either divine, diabolical, or simply human in source. It may be simply human in the same way as visual hallucination can be simply human, but more easily. The reason for this is that the "interior" voice may be nothing more than a very vivid auditory image—produced by and for the imagination, but not recognized as such because we rarely in fact attend to our auditory imagery. But that we can do so is evidenced, for example, by the fact that a trained musician can enjoy the melody while merely reading the score visually, or that any of us can hear with the mind's ear (and without humming a note) at least a portion of a familiar melody. As with visual imagery, so also with auditory, people's capacity varies enormously, and one should not estimate the possible intensity and vividness in either modality simply by thinking of one's own. Rather one should remember Socrates' daimonion, whose voice was so real to him that he followed its advice. Moreover, hearing voices is one of the regular symptoms of schizophrenia. To the schizophrenic, these voices are as real as a normal voice to a healthy person, or a "supernatural" voice to a visionary. That Socrates' daimonion may have been a schizophrenic phenomenon is borne out also by the evidence of his cataleptic trances. One does not wish to suggest that St. Joan of Arc's voices were also symptomatic of a schizoid personality (though it is possible that other phenomena in the saint's life might also be fitted into this picture). But it is important to remember that there is nothing intrinsically impossible or repugnant in thinking that Almighty God could and would make use of such a means to guide a chosen one—for the schizophrenic is a sick person, and the Lord certainly exalts the weak to confound the strong.

The content of hallucination, whether auditory or visual, will, like the dream content, always be found to be analyzable into elements of the subject's past experience, since all the content naturally in the mind will have come through the senses. It may, however, be found in bizarre combinations and structures, which may make it seem new or novel. The technique of dream analysis, apart from the interpretation of symbolic content, consists simply in tracing the dream-content to its original sensory source. If on occasion a vision (external or "imaginary") or an auditory hallucination can be shown to have a content demonstrably not derivable from the possible sensory experience of the subject (e.g., a vision of future events or an auditory hallucination in a language utterly unknown to the subject), then one has a negative criterion by which to rule out the human subjective source of the phenomenon, but not as yet a criterion by which to judge between a possible divine or diabolic source. But the fact that the total content of the image is derivable from the subject's own experience is not a positive criterion by which to establish a purely subjective human source, since it is conceivable that both divine and diabolic power could use the subject's own experience as the raw material for imagery. The decision as to whether a given phenomenon of this order is merely human or not is fairly easy and is best left to the combined judgment of theologians and psychiatrists. It is the theologian's task to pronounce on the moral content and effects of such phenomenon, but the psychiatrist's to decide whether or not the personality of the subject is such that these phenomena conform to what in his experience belong to the realm of pathological emotional states. If the moral content is unworthy of a divine source, the phenomenon is human in origin. But even if the moral content is beyond reproach, but the personality is such that phenomena of this kind might be expected, it is again reasonable to postulate a human source. But the decision as to whether it is divine or diabolic in origin is a more difficult question. The criteria usually accepted are (a) the type of personality who claims to have had such experience, (b) the content of the imagery, and (c) the effects on the spiritual and mental life of the subject. The first is important, but by no means final. A saint or a sinner can both be chosen for such favors. St. Paul was not a saint on the road to Damascus; the Curé of Ars was already saintly when he experienced diabolic manifestations. The second criterion we have already seen in one context, where it can be used negatively to rule out a merely human source. But it has another use: this time the moral or spiritual character of the content is involved. But here again it is of only limited value. If the moral or spiritual content of the imagery conflict with faith or morals, then its source cannot be divine. But the fact that the content from this point of view is irreproachable is not of itself a proof of divine origin. It may be merely human, and it is not impossible that the devil could produce such phenomena in order eventually to deceive. The third criterion involves a long time-process, and is not easily applied in any case. It will be seen from this paragraph that there is no easy way of deciding as to the origin of these phenomena. For that reason, the teaching of St. John of the Cross is very salutary. It can be summed up simply by saying that one should take no notice of visions and revelations, but live one's spiritual life on a basis of faith, hope and charity. If the alleged visions are divine, Almighty God will see to it if he wishes that this become abundantly clear. If they are not, then no harm will be done.

Some of the most difficult problems in psychopathology as well as in the realm of visions and revelations are presented by the hysterical personality. It should be noted that hysteria here does not mean simply the outbursts of emotions, floods of tears, and screams of terror associated with the popular notion of being "in hysterics." It is a form of illness of the personality (or, more accurately, of the emotions), whose manifestations are legion. We shall consider only two forms—hysterical anaesthesia and conversion hysteria. In the former sensation, or sensibility, is lost in a strictly limited field, without any discernible organic lesion. In the latter, the repressed emotion is converted into a physical symptom. (This is a picturesque and analogical way of describing a very difficult psychophysical process. It is the generally accepted formulation in psychiatry, and is adequate for our purposes.) The symptom produced can be almost anything—a pain in the back, laryngitis, coughing, headache, high temperature, insomnia, anaemia, loss of weight, etc., etc. But more to our purpose, it can be a visible lesion of the periphery. Dermatology and psychosomatic medicine generally is establishing ever more clearly and definitely the role of emotions in the aetiology of all sorts of disorders.

In the first type—hysterical anaesthesia—one is very close to the phenomena of rapture and ecstasy. No case of levitation through histeria is recorded in literature, so perhaps this phenomenon can be excluded. But trance, catalepsy, loss of sensibility, amnesia, loss of orientation and adaptation to environment, de-personalization, blindness, deafness, insensibility to pain, paralysis, rigidity, all these phenomena, and many others of visionaries, have their counterpart at least in the phenomena of hysteria.

With regard to conversion symptoms, the connection between hypnosis and hysteria must be borne in mind. Dissociation is characteristic of both phenomena. By this is meant (again in analogical and merely descriptive terms) the fact that a process or content ordinarily under the control or general supervision of consciousness is split off, as it were, and maintains a quasi-independent existence or functioning of its own. There is a case recorded in the literature where a patient was hypnotized (in deep trance), touched lightly on the forearm with a pencil and told she was being burnt; the spot touched was bandaged and sealed, and the patient kept under strict supervision through the night. Next morning a discernible mark was visible, closely resembling a slight burn. Add to this the fact that hysterics can produce physiological symptoms of the variety listed above, and one will not be surprised if occasionally alleged stigmatics are found to be hysterical personalities.

The intelligent Catholic layman, in the light of all this, will adopt caution as his watchword in all that belongs to the realm of visions and private revelations. In this he will be merely following the salutary advice of St. John of the Cross and the great St. Teresa, and also the universal practice of the shepherds of the flock at all times. Moreover, even when the Church does authenticate such phenomena they still do not belong to the realm of truths to be held on divine faith.

11 taboo, ritual and religion

Taboo is a Polynesian word for a phenomenon which is
almost universal. A taboo is a prohibition which depends for
its enforcement on horror, which itself is a mixture of fear,
self-loathing, dread of the unknown, revulsion, desire for
punishment, and perhaps other factors. Violation of the taboo
is so dreadful that no reason need be given for the taboo
itself or for the punishment which follows its violation.
Taboo operates at an emotional level so that the consequences of violation are not due to the culprit's being observed, charged, found guilty and punished, as it were from
without, but rather the evil result is intrinsic to the act of
violation itself. Taboo, because of its universality, belongs
to a deep level of the psyche, and it can take many forms.
Very often in primitive communities one finds a taboo on
certain foods either for the community as a whole, or for
some section of it. Certain persons may be taboo—the king
or priest—or the members of the group may be forbidden to
marry within their own group, or to marry outside their own
group. The universal incest taboo indicates how deeply this
type of taboo can reach into the human psyche. Certain
objects such as clothing, weapons, tools, may be taboo to

certain people, and their use allowed only to a privileged group.

One can parallel these taboo phenomena to some extent in our society, in minor and sometimes amusing ways. One can also find behavior or parallels in the practice of religion. A little careful observation of people around one will reveal interesting if sometimes trivial taboos. Thus, for example, consider snails as an item of diet in our culture. You will find traces of an emotional revulsion against the very idea. Again compare the reaction of a young boy with the many adults' reaction on touching a frog. The young boy has not yet learnt the taboo, and so feels no sense of revulsion or horror. Horseflesh is taboo meat in many countries. Elderberries are taboo in many parts of Ireland. Among actions, I should think that in our society there is a taboo on a girl's whistling in the street, and of course smoking in the street was taboo until comparatively recently. We also operate taboos on words: these taboo words vary from one generation to another. Many taboo words from Victorian times are now matters of everyday speech. Certain subjects are taboo in our society. The Crown perhaps, or more obviously the Coronation Stone, is taboo in Britain. These examples are not given as "pure" taboos but as areas where a more primitive, pre-rational type of thinking survives intermingled with other, more sophisticated elements.

Taboos are so widespread that it is reasonable to suppose that some very fundamental psychological process is at work. Taboo involves two things: the object or person who is taboo is at once sacred and dangerous. Because the thing or person is sacred, it is placed apart, and because it is dangerous it becomes attractive. Inevitably this generates an ambivalent attitude in the mind of the onlooker. More specifically, desire and aversion arise together in respect of the same object.

Desire and aversion can lead at one and the same time to reverence and dread. So you find a deep-seated conflict: on the one hand the movement to grasp or attain the object, because it is sacred and therefore desirable, and at the same time a deep-seated fear of the object and a reluctance to have anything to do with it, because it is dangerous. The result is a conflict of motives: on the one hand admiration and at the same time fear. This conflict occurs below the level of rational process, with the result that anxiety is generated. The function of this anxiety is the maintenance of social or public order. One can see modified forms of this taboo mechanism in, for example, the respect one has for a policeman or for a priest, or for the bus or theater queue. The relation between social control and taboo is roughly something like this: if you can create a thing or symbol which is so sacred as to need no explanation, and which procures horror at its violation, then you have a sufficient mechanism for the maintenance of a stable social organization. The divine right of kings theory was perhaps a survival of a taboo: the sacredness of kingship. Thus there were many revolutions in history, in which a king was overthrown, but not the monarchy itself. It took the French Revolution to overthrow at once the king, the monarchy and the taboo.

When one looks more closely at taboos one finds that they are in origin irrational—that is to say there is no rational justification, for example, for a taboo on meat, or, on miscegenation, or on certain words. Nevertheless, it is so.

Ritual is standardized overt behavior of a non-logical sort. Its function is either to purge the guilt incurred in the violation of the taboo, or to obtain favors from the deity, for example in fertility rites at the spring sowing. The rite performed is not the result of reflective thinking nor is it capable of itself of producing the desired result. It is not just repetitive stereotyped behavior. For example, polishing buttons in the army is not ritualistic behavior. But saying "Cheers" before a drink is. An elaborate stereotyped technological piece of behavior such as the checking of an aircraft before take-off is not ritual. To be a piece of ritual, the behavior must be socially imposed, it must satisfy emotional needs, *it must not of itself in the natural order be capable of achieving its intended result,* and it must involve a sense of control of unknown factors, where the real cause cannot be manipulated. Taboo incurred is cleansed by ritual, anxiety is allayed and security re-achieved. Thus taboo and ritual are complementary, for whereas the function of taboo is to generate anxiety, that of ritual is to produce a feeling of security.

The application of psychoanalytic concepts to anthropological phenomena, particularly in cultural anthropology, has now a history of perhaps fifty years behind it. The application of analytic concepts in this field was made by Freud himself in a series of works, *Totem and Taboo, The Future of an Illusion,* and *Moses and Monotheism.* In his *Obsessive Acts and Religious Practices* he put forward the theory that religious practice and the compulsive repetitive behavior of the neurotic were essentially the same phenomenon, and this concept he retained all his life. He was not an anthropologist, nor was he a social psychologist, but it is possible that he has given us here a suggestion, a partial insight into a truth which might well repay careful study by the theologian, the liturgist, and the moralist.

As Freud saw it, the study of primitive cultures, particularly the study of the taboo phenomenon and of ritual performances, threw considerable light on the nature and origins of religion itself, which he assumed was a "natural" phenomenon to be accounted for in psychological terms, and in the long run to be explained away as an "illusion". Freud used the word "primitive" in a sense of his own, and he used it consistently in this sense. He also used the word "natural" consistently, and in a sense of his own.

According to Freud, the potential reactions of the unconscious are "natural" to the child. When Freud says that something is natural to a child he means that it is a kind of primitive innate response which the child cannot help. Aggression therefore in Freud's sense is "natural" to the child. Freud equates the primitive with the natural, but not in the sense of the moral theologian, to whom it means the moral good. The natural primitive impulses of the child spring from the Id. The Id, the unconscious part of us, is unadapted to civilized life, just as the primitive noble savage in Freud's (or Rousseau's) conception is unadapted to life in society. So the Id, has to be shaped or molded—that means in practice that the primitive material, the potential reactions of the Id, must be banned for two reasons: first, it is incompatible with the state of man living in society (a notion that Freud perhaps learned from Darwinian evolutionary theory), so that the cravings of the Id motivated by the pleasure-pain principle are not suitable to civilized life but must become modified in order to become socially acceptable. The process of molding or banning the Id is one of the sources of religion. Secondly, the social seeks to maintain itself as a group. For this reason the individualistic reactions of the primitive Id have to be socialized and this socialization of the individualistic reactions is one of the sources of ethics. In addition to this the impulses from the Id, according to analytic theory, generate anxiety. And this they do whether they are released or curbed. Anxiety is also generated by the experience of aggression from without.

In order to cope with the anxieties thus generated, man

creates for himself certain defenses. These defenses begin in childhood and last and grow with the growth of the individual. Freud thought that religion had its origin in man's helplessness before his own instinctive fears within and the forces of nature without. (St. Paul also talks of fears within and dangers without.) Freud thought that religion belongs to an early stage of human development before man had learned to control his own internal fears and impulses and the forces of nature outside him. The affective states generated by fears that well up from within and that are provoked by the dangers without are coped with by the introduction of counter-affects. What this means is that we produce another set of emotions to cope with our fears, instead of coping with them rationally. The function of these counter-affects is to suppress and control the fear-producing elements which man finds he cannot cope with rationally.

At this stage according to Freud, an illusion is developed by man which is grounded in his own individual experiences as a child. As a child when he experienced danger, or uncontrollable fears, or things he could not understand, he went to his father as a source of strength and comfort. He also experienced his father and mother as sources of authority and of love and protection. The child discovers he can win affection by obeying the commands of his parents. He knows by experience that he will be rewarded if he is good and punished if he is not good. In Freud's view, "religion" derives from the fact that the adult regresses to his infantile experience and affective life when he comes up against danger or threats that he cannot cope with. Thus the adult approaches his deity for the same things for which the child approached his father. Freud thought that essentially religion was nothing but that, but he went further. Not only was religion a re-using of infantile patterns of behavior, but it was also a neurosis. The behavior of the child in seeking from his father relief from anxiety or defense against fears, is not neurotic. It is a natural primitive response and, because it is "natural", it is as it were right for the child. But a child's behavior is not "natural" to an adult and if the adult behaves in the child's way, his behavior is regressive and therefore neurotic. Freud thought therefore two things happened with the adult: in religion he ran for protection to God, who according to Freud is an illusion which we ourselves have created, and in addition the adult tries to placate his god, and to obey what he thinks are his deity's commands. Underlying this theory of Freud's is a fundamental principle of Freudian thought which is not made explicit in Freud's own writings but is tacitly assumed by him and by many of his followers. We owe its explicit formulation to Zilboorg. The principle can be put like this: where two behavior patterns are observed to exhibit the same constituents or are reducible to the same component elements they are due to the same psychological elements. Fromm points out that Freud himself saw the invalidity of this sort of reasoning, but I think it is true that in spite of this he fell into precisely this fallacy. Zilboorg calls it the fallacy of psycho-mechanistic parallelism. In a different terminology we could put it this way: Freud thought that if he observed similar or parallel patterns of behavior, therefore these two processes and two patterns of behavior were essentially identical. This identification of process in different behavior manifestations can of course be valuable. Thus it is a help to see the dream and the schizophrenic monologue as isomorphic processes, or to identify the same hysterical processes in anorexia, glove paralyses, psychogenic blindness, and the wounds of some stigmatists.

Freud pointed out that one can observe parallels between the child, the neurotic and the religious person. He also believed that the child's affective factors generating other counter-affects were paralleled in the so-called religious person, who generates his own god and then worships him. In addition Freud thought that he had discovered certain parallels between the behavior of neurotic people and the behavior of religious people.

These parallels briefly were: (a) a sense of guilt is common to both, (b) a sense of dependence is common to both, (c) repetitive stereotyped compulsive pieces of behavior are common to both.

He drew two conclusions: one, that religion could be explained by the adult's regression to the child's affective states, and second, that the practices of religion were neurotic patterns of behavior because some of these patterns could be paralleled by certain behavior patterns of neurotic people. Thus a neurotic person will carry out a piece of behavior in great detail and with great regularity in a repetitive obsessional way and will feel uncomfortable if he does not go through with the action in the same set pattern time and time again. He thought this ritualistic performance of the neurotic individual was the same as the repetitive behavior of a religious person saying his prayers, for example, or carrying out a rite of religion. And both of neurotic behavior and the religious behavior seemed to him to be essentially identical with the ritualistic performances related to taboos, which characterized "primitive" people, whether children or aboriginal Australians. Again religion imposes certain prohibitions on its members and declares certain things, persons, or objects to be sacred, and thus set apart, rendered untouchable, or at any rate separated from the vulgar herd. This process or mechanism resembled in Freud's mind, the taboo mechanism in primitive cultures. Thus we can add ritual and taboo to the initial infantile neurotic regression in which religion, according to Freud, had its source.

We might perhaps put this more simply by considering for a moment the notion of guilt. For Freud, as for many psychologists and psycho-analysts, guilt is used in a rather special sense—a sense in which it always refers to neurotic guilt, or more accurately the sense in which guilt is always neurotic. For the Catholic, especially for the Catholic theologian, this of course is not so. The Catholic psychologist distinguishes two kinds of guilt; on the one hand neurotic guilt, and on the other rational guilt. Neurotic guilt is a complex state of the emotions in which one can distinguish fear, dread, self-loathing, anxiety, desire, sadness, sorrow, and perhaps a tinge of despair. Rational guilt, on the other hand, is the judgment one makes about oneself, in full consciousness, that one did something voluntarily, knowing that it was wrong. This sort of judgment can be and ideally should be devoid of the emotions connected with neurotic guilt. In practice, however, because of the complexity of human nature, and because of the fact that our behavior is rarely if ever entirely rational, the normal state of affairs for most people is a judgment of rational guilt, plus a carryover of some of the elements of "neurotic" guilt, in the form of emotional overtures, in almost infinitely varying degrees of intensity.

On the assumption however that all guilt is neurotic, Freud thought that religion must be considered as a means of getting rid of neurotic guilt, on the one hand by placating "god"—the projected father-image—and on the other hand by ritual cleansing of the guilt incurred by violation of taboo. Our problem here is to see how the processes or mechanisms of taboo and ritual resemble—if they resemble—the processes and practices of true religion, and how they differ—

if indeed they differ—from the practices and processes of true religion.

There is no reason to suppose that all that analytic theory has revealed about the genesis of religion is false. Nevertheless it must be said that some of the conclusions arrived at do not follow from the alleged evidence. If one begins with atheism, of course, no religion is either possible or healthy. It is worth noting in this regard that Freud's atheism was antecedent to his analytic theories, and not a consequence of them. He has, however, helped us to gain a valuable insight into the child's and the adolescent's attitude to God, and to understand a great *deal more about atheism* than was possible half a century ago. In a similar way, an understanding of ritual and taboo may help us a great deal in understanding many of the phenomena of religon which at first glance may appear unnecessary, incidental, or accidental. Thus, we may ask, why do we have ritual in the church? why sacraments? why such ceremonies as "churching" of women after childbirth?

The study of social psychology, like that of analytic theory, has also a history of more than half a century behind it, and again like analytic theory, it can be a valuable asset to the theologian studying the nature of the Church. Unlike analytic theory, however, it is only in recent years that social psychology has achieved anything like the status of a science. One of the laws in Freudian theory was the tacit assumption that one could understand both the individual and society through a study of "individual" psychology. Social psychology is interested in the functional aspect of the group considered precisely as a group, and not as a collection of individuals. Any form of conduct which occurs in the group, is determined by the group, and is not found outside the group, belongs to the realm of social psychology. There is a sense in which everything one does, except idiosyncratic processes and simple responses, will be socially determined, so that it is difficult sometimes to draw the line between individual and social psychology. But the critic or art historian can determine in the individual work certain elements which place it as the work of a particular region, period, or school. These elements are part of a social operation, and not the work of one individual *per se.* Again, the behavior of an individual in danger, or faced with a threat of war, or in seeking recreation in leisured moments, will be his own individual choice perhaps, but precisely what he does may be due to the preferred persistent tendencies of the group. The Church is a *coetus hominum,* a group of men. Whatever belongs to the psychological nature of a group as such may be expected to hold of the group which is the Church (excluding such elements, if there are any, which are incompatible with her divine origin, but including all that is "natural" to the group, in the theologian's meaning of natural). Moreover just as other natural elements (water, oil, salt) have been taken over by her Divine Founder, and elevated to an efficacy and a function which they could not have had of their own nature, so one might expect to find that the "natural" elements of society have been taken over and elevated in a similar and analogous way. Thus, in every society one can discern hierarchical structure and differentiation of function. These in turn are found in the Church in a two-fold way. On the one hand her essential structure (pope, bishops, and other orders) is of divine origin, the necessary hierarchical structure of any organization of men being transmitted into something far higher, while there still remain other structures and differentiations (e.g., sub-groups within the Church, each with its own organization) of human origin.

Ritual and taboo are at once phenomena of psychology,

social psychology, and cultural anthropology. They have not so far received the attention they deserve from the theologian. In what follows it will be contended that these "natural" elements of human conduct so far from proving the "natural" origin of religion, can throw considerable light on the actuality of the Church divinely constituted "for us and for our salvation".

The argument of the psychologist and the cultural anthropologist may now be put in fairly simple terms: We generate our god through projecting our infantile father-image. We need our god because our earthly father has failed us. We have become anxious through a violation of taboo (which we think of as moral fault) and so we need a cleansing mechanism to rid ourselves of our intolerable sense of guilt.

This argument is applied to religion in the following form: our religion is only one among many. It involves certain taboos such as food laws (meat on a Friday, fasting regulations) or sexual prohibitions. Objects are declared sacred, so the faithful must not touch a chalice. It involves ritualistic performances: such as the rite of the Holy Sacrifice, the rites of administration of the sacraments, repetitive prayers such as the Rosary. Thus morals become, as with Russell, simply the violation of primitive taboos. And the Mass and the sacraments become irrational devices for cleansing us of our primitive anxieties generated by our violation of our primitive taboos. Thus the whole of religion becomes a pre-rational, or sub-rational operation, and together with the antecedent wiping out of God, becomes something meaningless and unworthy of adult manhood. This is the doctrine which many of our people and those of other religions are made to imbibe at the hands of many university teachers and popular authors. What is to be said of it?

Let me try to state some preliminary points first. It is

assumed by the exponents of this line of teaching that there is nothing in man, in mature man, that is not sensory or emotional in character. Thus the fact that rational processes of thought differ in kind from those of the emotions and the senses is ignored or denied by those who hold the theory I am examining. But if there are no processes in man other than irrational ones, what is the point of trying to bring a sick mind from a condition in which it is at the mercy of irrational forces into a condition wherein reason can control these irrational forces? Yet this is precisely what a deep analysis is aimed at producing, in whatsoever language this idea may be expressed. It is hardly likely that the process of rehabilitation in analysis is simply the substituting of one set of emotional and irrational factors for another. In other words, the practice of analysis belies its theoretical formulation. Again, it is assumed that where two processes parallel each other, they are the same process. This is the fallacy already referred to under the title of psycho-mechanistic parallelism. The *facts* here are that the process of taboo and of moral prohibition parallel each other in some respects. The *conclusion* is therefore that they are the same process. As well might one argue that the processes of science and magic parallel each other in some respects and are therefore the same thing. Evans-Pritchard has shown in his classic *Witchcraft among the Azande* that the thought processes of those who practice magic and of those who practice science are parallel. Both involve the concept of cause and effect, both involve the logical process of arguments from consequences, both involve consistence and coherence, etc. But if the argument from parallelism of process holds in the one instance, it should hold also in the other, viz., that magic and science are the same thing. But no one would draw this conclusion, I think.

Now it is agreed that rational processes are not the same as sensory or emotional processes (and if there is any doubt about this, the experimental evidence of the Wurzburg group can be appealed to), and that parallelism of psychological process does not establish identity of content, we can take the next step.

The problem of the existence of God is not a problem in psychology or in cultural anthropology, but in metaphysics. Accepting that God exists and that he can be shown to exist, can one say that he could not if he so wished communicate with man: that is that He could not have made a revelation to man concerning truths which man could not have known otherwise? or even concerning truths which he could have come to know through natural means? This type of question is familiar to the theologian who deals with the *fontes revelationis,* and to the scripture scholar in connection with exegetical problems. The answer, on the plane of man's cognitive processes, has long been familiar. Almighty God could and did communicate with man. He could have done so through sensory channels (Our Divine Lord speaking and preaching) or through the imagination (visions, dreams etc.) or directly to the intelligence (the prophets, perhaps, or St. John). Assuming that such a revelation was in fact made, it would clearly have been made in accordance with man's capacity to receive, as well as in accordance with God's will to reveal. A true religion would not have been something out of all proportion to man's capacities and the exigencies and processes of his psyche. On the cognitive plane there is no real difficulty. We must examine the pre-rational, affective plane.

The assumptions of Freud of those who follow him in his thinking about the problems under consideration here, are somewhat as follows: if it can be shown that religion, and *a fortiori* our own religion, is related to man's needs, and takes account at once of his rational and sub-rational processes, or that his sub- or pre-rational processes are still catered for and discernible in it, it is not a true religion. Or to put it another way, the assumption seems to be that if *per impossibile* there were such a thing as a true religion, it would have to be something wholly removed from the human condition. On the contrary, our argument here is that if there were a true religion, precisely because it was a matter of divine revelation *to man,* we should expect to find in it just those elements demanded by our needs and constitution.

It is worth trying to make this even more explicit. Suppose it is true, as it very possibly is true, that we need some defenses against our infantile fears which stay with us at an unconscious level into adulthood. Suppose moreover that anxiety-generating taboos are in fact universal, and that some cleansing rituals are necessary to restore our primitive emotional security. Suppose moreover that these primitive taboos involve conceptions, such as the incest taboo, which have far-reaching genetic significance which a primitive mind could not form explicitly. Suppose that a form of social control is necessary to the survival of primitive society, and that rational factors and controls are not yet sufficient to ensure this (they are not sufficient even in more advanced societies). All these suppositions may in fact be true. Even if individuals may at different times and places have emancipated themselves from such pre-rational processes, it is quite clear that not all men have yet done so, and clear also that many of the processes of society are non-rational. It is further clear that since a society is by definition a society of men, and since man is not wholly rational, human society will not be wholly rational either. A revelation made in these circumstances, and a society even of divine origin founded in these circumstances will certainly take account of these phenomena. In terms of analytic theory itself, a revelation, if it is made, will be made in accordance with what man is, viz., a creature who needs defenses against his infantile fears, who needs to have his taboos reinforced, who needs pre- or sub-rational controls to ensure his successful achievement of full status as a man, and who needs the pre-rational processes of ritual to cleanse him of irrational guilt and anxiety.

One will expect therefore to find the successful use of these mechanisms, just as one might have expected the use of other "natural" material (speech, singing, bodily posture) elevated and transmuted to a higher significance.

These considerations may become clearer, perhaps, if one considers the nature of marriage. Human beings are motivated by the reproductive instinct, whether it be called libido, sex, or concupiscence. This is not removed but transmuted into something, not divorced from or unrelated to the primitive pre-rational process, by the fact of the sacrament of matrimony. The pre-rational and rational elements remain, both in motivation and behavior, but elevated into a channel of grace. In a similar way, the cleansing of water, the soothing of oil, remain while the sacramental efficacy of Baptism and Anointing is achieved by the use of these natural objects, plus ritual (the "form"). If in addition to ritual and taboo, we are so constituted that we need symbols as well (and this is the contention of both Freud and Jungian theory, as well perhaps as being the result of the interdependence of sense and intellect) we have all three elements taken care of in the *res et sacramentum*.

It is not the formal function of religion as such to relieve us of our anxieties, but rather to glorify God, to enable us to express our finiteness and dependence, to return thanks for the gift of existence. But if we need some means whereby to relieve ourselves of our primitive infantile pre-rational anxieties, and if we would have had recourse in any case to some ritualistic performances in order to do so, if moreover we must needs confess our conscious rational guilt as well, and make atonement for it, as well as protesting (symbolically in sacrifice) our finiteness, is it surprising that in one and the same act, for instance in the Holy Sacrifice, we should achieve all these purposes simultaneously? This is really divine economy.

One can perhaps see something of the transmutation of the pre-rational in some of the ritual observances of the Old Testament. Scripture scholars have little difficulty in accepting the code of Hammurabai as a forerunner of the decalogue: on the one hand a pre-existing code (similar perhaps to Hammurabai's) may have been "canonized", or perhaps the natural law itself elevated to divine positive law. Similarly, the taboos (unclean animals, menstruating women) of a primitive tribe become part of the law of Moses. Ritual washing, which is enjoined in many religions, may very well represent our need for expiation through cleansing from the horror incurred by violation of taboo, at a pre-rational level. There would appear to be no difficulty in accepting the fact that Almighty God has in these instances subsumed the pre-rational, through the rational, into the supernatural. Can we see anything similar in the Church?

The fact that one finds in religion, or in the practice of it, phenomena which closely parallel the phenomena of ritual and taboo, does not establish the identity of two sets of phenomena. Such an identification would involve the fallacy already referred to as psycho-mechanistic parallelism. But that they should be closely related should not be surprising. One should in fact expect such parallels, since Christ in the words of St. John "knew what was in man", and made provision for it. The taboo element survives in food laws and fasting laws, in not touching the sacred vessels, in bareheaded women in church, in the crime of sacrilege, the inviolability of sacred persons, and in many other respects. But that is not to say that such laws are *mere* taboos, any more than marriage is mere mating-behavior. They cater for our primitive needs (the horror element), for our rational needs (for order), and for our supernatural needs (discipline, mortification, reverence).

The ritual element survives in all our corporate acts of worship. But more to the point here, it survives in ritual washing (Baptism, washing before Mass, and at the lavabo), in purification rites (exorcism, churching,) in symbolism (candles, incense, sign of the cross), in oral (repetitive) prayer etc. Again, that is in no sense to say that these processes are *nothing but* primitive rituals: they also, like taboos, have a multiple significance. They serve to reassure, to relieve emotional pressures, to allay anxiety at the pre-rational level. At the rational level, they are significant means of symbolic expressions of our conscious thought processes, which otherwise might approximate to the "ineffable", and supernaturally, they are blessings, acts of worship, signs of grace. It is this multiple signification which eludes the non-believing psychologist. But we ourselves should be careful not to repudiate such multiple signification. We do not in fact repudiate it, but we sometimes perhaps shy away from calling it what it is: a combination of pre-rational ritual and taboo mechanisms with rational and supernatural elements. Need one add that of course the supernatural elements are the most important, and that one should progressively try to eliminate all that is merely pre-rational from one's personal involvement: this is part of the purification of intention of the spiritual writers. One has met priests who, on occasion of illness or traveling, found it impossible to say Mass. In the uneasy feeling, the sense of non-rational guilt incurred in such circumstances, may one discern something of the pre-rational guilt feeling of primitive thinking? In the anxiety experienced by a good Catholic who inadvertently eats meat on a Friday and though knowing that no sin was committed, feels constrained to confess the violation ("you feel better after telling the priest"), can one not discern a survival of primitive violation of taboo: the guilt incurred even by total innocence, provided only that the taboo is violated. This was the "guilt" of Oedipus.

We are very close to the irrational in our minds and lives. There is ever present to Christians individually a danger that they (as distinct from the body corporate of the Church) may import into the practice of their religion elements even more closely related to primitive ritual and taboo mechanisms. Our attitude to sacred things may regress from reverence to ambivalent fear and dread. Our method of prayer may take on a repetitive compulsive character analagous to neurotic behavior. Our use of the sacramentals such as medals, holy pictures, even holy water, may resemble all too closely the use of charms, talismans, and sympathetic magic. One can see extreme examples of such regressions in the "cults" which spring up from time to time in under-developed areas where Christianity, through lack of adequate instruction, deep roots, or sufficient priests, degenerates into superstition.

I have been arguing that one should expect to find in Christianity some of the elements of primitive taboo and ritual, but transmuted, as the mating of animals in marriage, or the efficacy of cleansing by water in Baptism. One may ask how do ritual and taboo in the purely anthropological sense *differ* from the practices of true religion. The answer is fairly simple. First, taboos are *in themselves* non-rational prohibitions, even if *what* they prohibit (e.g., incest) should be prohibited anyway on rational grounds. Moral precepts are, however, "ordinances of reason". Thus some moral precepts and some taboo prohibitions will coincide, others not. Second, taboo operates through deep irrational horror and fear, morals through conscious judgment. But again, the two may coincide, for example, in the horror experienced by some at the guilt incurred by sexual sin, or they may diverge, so that the horror and dread may exist without actual sin ("neurotic guilt"), may exist without any emotional concomitant. Thirdly, ritual performances in the anthropological sense are incapable of achieving the desired result (e.g., a fertility rite and an abundant harvest), while the sacramental rites of the Church by divine institution are of themselves efficacious.

Clearly there is a great deal more research to be done in this and allied fields. Analytic theory has already done us the great service of helping us to understand why many people reject the faith. It could do us the further great service, if we study it adequately, of enabling us constantly to purify our faith and our practice of it of all unworthy elements.

12 society, identity and change

It is just about half a century since McDougall published his *Social Psychology;* and it is curious to reflect how closely related this work is to the social psychology of its time. It grew out of the thinking of its era: an era which took for granted its own stability, and the permanence of its mores. Thus it was impossible to assume that the behavior of the group could be accounted for, explained, even explained away, by tracing each unit of behavior back to some primordial and unchanging "instinct". It would be amusing, but unprofitable, to trace these ideas to their source: Rousseau, perhaps, the French Enlightenment, Hobbes, Hume. The ancestry is noble, if legion and somewhat dispersed. It is also just about half a century since Freud attempted from his rather special point of view to comprehend social process. The origins of his thinking may have been different, but the tacit assumption was the same as that of McDougall: both from opposite poles assumed that one could understand the behavior of both the individual and of society by understanding "individual" psychology. The great reform movements, the Enlightenment, the Spencer-Bentham-Mill axis of social thinking, down to and including Fabianism and the Webbs, the European brand of socialism, and the Hegelian-

Marxist political philosophy—all assumed and based their thinking on a social psychology which only reached formal expression in McDougall and Freud—each from his own particular point of view, each perhaps thinking how remote he really was from the other. But the *bellum omnium contra omnes* is at once McDougall's instinct of pugnacity and Freud's death-wish, the destructive instinct, the aggression of the Id, (as it is also Trotter's herd-instinct at war); life, liberty and the pursuit of happiness is McDougall's parental and sex-impulse instinct, as it is Freud's eros, the ultimate end and purpose of all ego-processes, and indeed the very reason for the generation of the ego. Otherwise the Id would have it all its own way and we should never have emerged from Hobbes', Locke's, or Rousseau's pre-social condition.

It was a pity that for such a long time, and during so much psychological theorizing about man and society both the nature of man and of society were so largely ignored. The fact that man can be rational and behave rationally was ignored by some, and the fact that society can be irrational and moved, perhaps primarily, by irrational forces was ignored by others. Social change planned on the basis of a wholly rational man has a long lineage, from Plato to the most recent of contemporary Utopias: it underlay the concept of Economic Man and the Utilitarian concepts of the nineteenth century, as it also underlay Hegel and his descendents in fascism or marxism. It was disappointing to discover that *"naturam expelles furca, tamen, usque recurret"*. For there is an inherent dialetic between man and society. Man is at once a person, who rises above society, and an individual of a species, one among many, often perhaps lost among many. In his capacity of person, he is rational, unique, incommunicable, responsible. But in his capacity of membership of the species, he is animal, sensory, merged and molded. Society also presents this dualism: it is at once rational, in all the ways in which society differs from herd, and non-rational where the individual gets lost in the species.

Social psychology must retain this multiple and complex viewpoint if it is not to degenerate into silly oversimplifications. For perhaps the greatest fallacy of all is the fallacy of assuming that the principle of parsimony, a valid principle of methodology in the sciences of matter, should hold also in the sciences of man. It would be amusing to trace all the varieties of explanation offered for man's behavior by the application of this principle: instinct, evolution, conditional reflexes, Kohler's apes, libido, cybernetics, ribonucleic acid, each in turn was a one-principle solution, and each in turn though containing some truth, was inadequate. The complexity remained and demanded a complex explanation.

The group does not explain man the person, nor does man the individual explain the group. Each is a phenomenon worth studying in its own right, and each needs an explanation appropriate to itself. Social psychology must presume its own raw material, its object of study, as any other science must do, but it has to determine for itself which precise aspect or dimension of the raw material is its competence. Man-in-society is the raw material. Man-in-himself, the person, is the object of other specialties within the science of psychology. What man ought to do, how the person ought to behave, it is not the competence of the social psychologist to determine. The basis of the Kinsey ethic, or more recently the Reith Lectures ethic is something like this: go and find out what man in society is doing. Then tell him that is what he ought to be doing. This is a curious reversal of the old story of the mother who sent her friend to find out what little John was doing, "and tell him he mustn't". It bases its ethical relativity on a doctrine of cultural relativity, which in turn depends on social psychology. It is of course imperative to plan for social change on the basis of a thorough knowledge of the facts. And social psychology can contribute greatly to our understanding of the facts. But how can one plan for change merely on the basis of a knowledge of the present or past facts? Nothing follows about the values of the facts from their mere recording. No plan for the future emerges merely from a listing, nor even from a listing plus adequate understanding or conceptualization of the facts. Both the evaluation, and the choice of plan for the future depend on matters other than the mere recording of present fact. One plans for the future, one plans a change in society, because for some reason the change is seen as better than that which pre-existed it. Thus, good inter-race relations are better than strife and genocide. Social welfare and well-being are better than poverty and suffering, social and international peace are better than war. One may, one must, ask why? And the answer, whatever it may be, will not be just another proposition from one or other of the empirical sciences. Social psychology thus cannot determine our goals for us. But it must have its own goals. These are the understanding of the behavior of groups, and the changes in the behavior of the individual because he is a member of a group—in a word, the functional aspect of groups of human beings considered precisely as groups, and not as individuals. I say human beings, because although it is interesting to study bees or ants, or colonies of white rats, and may even be profitable in unexpected ways, these groups only analogously merit the term societies. It is precisely in the ways in which human behavior in groups differs from the stereotyped behavior of bees that it becomes interesting. Lorenz, Tinbergen, Klopfer, have done fascinating work, but it does not help us to plan for social change—except perhaps by counterpointing the differences. For in respect of human society, at any rate, Heraclitus was right. Its reality *is* change.

We have no knowledge of a wholly static society, but only of societies subject to greater or less rate of change. The difference between ourselves and the great social reformers of the past lies perhaps in this that we have the tools with which to try to comprehend the nature of the changes society undergoes, to channel these changes to ends we determine as desirable, to offset the effects of undesirable ends, and particularly to take avoiding action now to prevent the onset of evils which through lack of knowledge in the past could not perhaps have been prevented, but which, if they should occur in our case, will be unpardonable. We have a moral obligation, deriving from the professional status we claim, to equip ourselves with the kind of knowledge, the insights, now available so that evils may be avoided. This means of course that planning for the future demands a knowledge of the past. It has been rightly said that he who knows no history is condemned forever to relive it. Adequate understanding of the past, enormous research into the present, these are indispensable prerequisites for the social psychologist.

His science, however, is still in its infancy, almost as it were, still in gestation, after the false starts or miscarriages of the past.

Any form of conduct which occurs in the group, is determined by the group, and is not found outside the group, belongs to the realm of social psychology. There is even a sense in which everything one does except idiosyncratic processes and simple responses, will be socially determined, so that it is difficult sometimes to draw the line between social and individual psychology. The critic or art historian can determine in the individual work—and what can be more individualistic than a great work of art—certain elements which place it as the work of a particular region or epoch, period or school. These elements are part of a social operation, and not the work or choice of any one individual in isolation. Undoubtedly, the contribution of the individual is of paramount and overriding importance. But it is also important, though in a more modest way, to discover, if we can, the social determinants. This in a sense is the task the social psychologist takes on himself. The behavior of an individual in danger, faced with the threat of war, seeking recreation in leisured moments, choosing his clothes, or his attitudes to other groups (other nations, religions, or sub-groups), deciding on a determinate course of action (to send a son to the University, to expand production, to call a strike), may in large measure be his own individual choice, but it will also be affected to some extent by the pressures of the groups to which he belongs, both peer groups and reference groups. The group pressures affect him as an individual of the species (or, in this case, sub-species). But the final choice is the choice of a person. Cultural relativists, of all kinds, and some totalitarian social psychologists take account only of the pressures on the individual of the species. Should the pressures be of such magnitude that they issue directly in behavior, the individual is not responsible for the acts ensuing. This is the beehive concept. But this is rare in human affairs. Mob violence, mass panic in a theater fire, perhaps the social pressures of the Revolutionary Colleges in China for many approximate to this condition. But the more usual state of affairs is that the pressures are processed through the ego, through the conscious personality of the individual, and thus behavior, for better or worse, becomes conduct. Bees do not conduct themselves, they behave. The great mystery of all conduct is social conduct, as General Smuts has said.

The political, social, economic, legal and religious organization of the community, and specific institutions such as the family, the school and the factory provide the living framework within which the process of human development takes place. The sociologist's study of these phenomena provides the basis for the social psychologist's understanding of the interplay of the rational and non-rational elements in socially determined conduct. There is a reciprocal causality between the culture of the group and the personality of its members: the culture produces the kind of person the society seeks to produce, and the members of the society produce the kind of culture they deserve. Very often neither of these processes is fully articulate in any member of the group. This is particularly the case in relatively unsophisticated and highly traditional groups. And even in the most highly sophisticated self-conscious and mobile groups, it will be clear only to the minority.

The members of the group will constantly wonder what is it that makes them a group. They will repeat over and over the one element or item their society has taught them to identify with, as though it were explanatory of their survival and functioning as a group. This may range from blood, soul, or language, or territorial limits to the nazionsgeist, zeitgeist, or the march of God through the world as in a Hegelian Prussia. Always the search as before will be for the one unit which will explain all. And always the social psychologist will try to point out that it is never any one item. The law of parsimony does not hold. Unlike the sciences of matter, the aesthetic pleasure of simplicity or elegance is not a criterion of acceptability of a hypothesis. Whatever it is that constitutes a group, which turns it into a viable entity through time, is an amalgam of many factors. The total culture produces and is intended to produce an image of the society whose culture it is, through which a chosen set of attitudes, emotions, and habits of thought and action are transmitted to the next generation, where in principle they are absorbed but always with some sifting (and this is the basis of social change), or to the incoming member from another society, who succeeds only in part in assimilating them, no matter how much he may try. One cannot in adulthood become an Englishman, an Irishman or a Frenchman. A culture in this sense involves the arts, sciences and technology of the group, the religious and philosophical beliefs and values, the political institutions and practices, the habits of daily life, the public rituals and taboos together with a set of preferred persistent tendencies common to the group. The preferred persistent tendencies are the most important factors; it is they in the long run which mold the group and which turn the group into a nation. The constituents of the culture in this sense are transmitted to the members of the group by all the channels of communication estabished between one generation and the next: all the channels of education, both unstructured and formalized. The unstructured includes the parent-child relationship, play activity, public pronouncement, newspapers, literature, etc. The formal refers to schools, church, etc. A large segment of the content of the culture in this sense will be non-rational. It will consist of myths, prejudices and stereotypes, false beliefs, and illegitimate or unattainable aspirations. The non-rational, false or unethical dimensions of these elements will be carefully concealed or rationalized by the assumption that they are right and just for no other reason than that the group sanctions them.

Any suggestion of change in the beliefs of the group about itself (i.e., in its accepted self-image) meets with strong opposition, as witness the Athenians' rejection of Socrates on a charge of impiety. And yet the self-image of the group embodied in its preferred persistent tendencies is changing

all the time. This is one source of the inevitable tension between the generations in a mobile society. The more the
society is subject to change, the more will the self-image
change, and with it the real content of the culture. This will
be recognized earlier by members of the younger group,
whose self-image is still plastic, who are still in process of
forming their self-image of the culture. They will find it at
variance with the image projected by the older age group;
in other words they will find the real image communicated
by life at variance with the projected or ideal one communicated by the devices of the society itself. This is true in the
religious as well as in the secular sphere. The conflicts experienced by the second generation immigrant in the United
States are a clear example of the type of conflict which occurs
between the generations in any highly mobile society.

Western society is in a highly mobile phase at present.
In fact it is going through a deep and far-reaching cultural
revolution. We shall expect to find the processes outlined
above verified in our midst now or in the very near future.
Perhaps what we need most at present is to examine the
social institutions, beliefs, practices, and taboos in our midst,
with a view to seeing which of them are merely man-made,
and which are not changeable, which could be altered without undue loss, and which embody real values. There is no
way known to man whereby a culture can be preserved intact, while at the same time remaining a living thing. One
can put a culture in a museum, or preserve it, like classical
antiquity, in books and the minds of scholars. But if there
is one thing known with certainty by the social psychologist,
it is simply this: that a culture is something lived, not pickled;
and life means change. It is interesting to try to list the major
elements of change in our culture. I do not mean such passing
trivialities as dress or slang, and which are sometimes con-

noted by the term cultural change. I mean the far-reaching changes in the self-image of a people, the transition from a horizontally unstratified society to a highly stratified one, from a lived christianity perhaps to a post-christian society, the switch from national to international interest, from conditions of no leisure in one geneation to holidays abroad in the next, from acceptance of traditional values and beliefs to their total rejection as with Joyce, from subsistence level farming to the affluent society, from a peasant-structured and institutionalized society to a middle class way of life, and all this in one or two generations. True, many things have not changed. Many things ought not to change. But by trying to prevent change in areas where it is right and desirable to prevent it, as it is for instance right and desirable in the sphere of genuine values and truths, are we trying, like King Canute, to hold back the tide? Have we confused the unessential in our culture with the essential? Are we therefore in danger of alienating our young people from the real values of our culture by asking them to accept an all-or-nothing version of the culture? Have we made the greatest mistake of all in this context, the mistake of confusing our faith with the dimensions of Western culture?

Our faith is essentially trans-culturally viable, since redemption is for all mankind. Have we taught a culture-bound version of it to our young people, particularly to our young intellectuals, and is this perhaps the reason why they have rejected it? Have we even done worse? Have we through fear created the illusion that the intellectual life itself is a danger to the faith? This latter is tragically false.

Even in our all-or-nothing concept there are difficulties and confusion. While our verbal formulations would sometimes seem to indicate that we advocate an all-or-nothing point of view, our own behavior in respect of the culture often belies the formulations we give it. Even those who are most keen on the impossible, the pickling of a culture, which can only result in its death, have themselves changed without recognizing the fact.

In the context of the new Europe, or of a world society, the fear is often expressed that the smaller nations will "lose their national identity" in the wider society of Europe. This is a subtle but unreal fear. It corresponds in society to the fear of loss of identity on the part of the schizophrenic. The way to preserve one's identity is to accept the facts of change, growth, and development. The way to lose it is to try to preserve it unchanged. Paradoxically, a way of life must be trans-culturally viable if it is to survive as a culture, because the basic human problems and their solutions are in their broad outline essentially the same everywhere. A culture cannot be identified with any one item within it. It is an organized whole. It hangs together, and the whole pattern changes simultaneously, though perhaps imperceptibly, like the living organism itself.

Perhaps the most important discovery of the social psychologist is this: if one tampers with one item in a whole culture pattern, one may destroy the whole picture, the unity of the culture. Here is where the social psychologist has an important role to play in our society. A culture exists in three dimensions, the intellectual, the ceremonial, and the material. The intellectual dimension refers to all the belief, values, traditions, the arts, sciences, religion and philosophy of a people. The ceremonial refers to the accepted and stylized modes of behavior, dress, and the symbolic processes of intercommunication, whether in language as understood in dictionaries or language in the wider sense of any meaningful unit of behavior. The material dimension refers to the instruments, tools, technology, material resources, property, housing, communications in the sense of roads and transport. And all three hang closely together in an intelligible construct, a way of life. The ceremonial culture often outlines changes in the other dimensions, as is seen for instance in the survival of monarchy in a culture where all the other dimensions have changed radically. The material dimension is usually the easiest to change, though there are exceptions to this. Moreover, if one wishes to change the intellectual and ceremonial dimensions, the surest way to do this is to change the material basis. This is the whole history of technology and its relation to culture.

But the important point is that one cannot radically change the material culture and hope to preserve all the rest intact. Yet this is the dilemma of our time. We have set in train certain great and far-reaching processes within the material culture which inevitably will have great and far-reaching effects in the other dimensions of the culture, have already had such effects. But while we are anxious to achieve the desirable changes in the material culture, we are reluctant to accept the other changes these inevitably bring with them. Resistance to change is of course understandable; it is a valuable element in bringing about a stable society, and of preserving the values and traditions of a culture or a way of life. But it can lead to an unhealthy conservatism. This is especially the case when the resistance to change is manifested as a resistance to change because it is change. No one perhaps would actually formulate his attitude in these words. But operatively that is how many of us behave. Resistance to change is due more often to non-rational factors than to rational ones. The non-rational factors are usually emotional. We do not like the source from which the suggestion of change comes, or we are full of fear of the change itself because we do not comprehend it, or we are fearful of some discomfort which the change may introduce, or we are simply afraid of the unknown in a primitive childish way. We may also resist change through not understanding its purpose, or more selfishly because we cannot see any short term gain in it for ourselves, and we are incapable of thinking ahead to the possible gains for others, even for our own children or the community at large. On the whole, lack of understanding, bad communications, and suspicion, prejudice or hatred would be a fair summary of the reasons why resistance to change is so widespread. Good and desirable changes, such as increased automation in industry, must be planned for, not just reluctantly allowed to happen. Its consequences must be anticipated and allowances made for the dislocations inevitable in a transition period. But to resist automation because of the fear of its consequences for human beings is an irrational fear. So far from its entailing our subjection to the machine, or our reduction to the level of morons, it should be a liberating process, conducive to the double release of man—of his organism from the burden of sheer muscular or routine repetitive work, and his mind from the forces of the irrational. Many cannot see this. They are unwittingly committed to the doctrine of Rousseau (which they confuse with Christianity) that technological advance is a retrograde step for man.

The social psychologist must be encouraged to look to the future, to try to extrapolate from present observed phenomena to the likely consequence of these. Education and services of all kinds must be planned for now, to meet the needs that the changes already introduced into our society will bring about. Burke's concept of the slow organic growth of social institutions is a sound one. But if the growth seems at times to resemble Jack's beanstalk rather than a slow organic process, one cannot afford to wait. One must act now to make sure that we will create the kind of society we want, and not incur the reproach of future generations, that we allowed evil to grow, or that we destroyed the good by not anticipating its consequences.

One cannot change the economic underpinning of a way of life, the self-image of a nation, and its role in international affairs without accepting, as a necessary concomitant, radical and far-reaching consequences in the structure and culture of the society itself. The good and necessary objective values of any culture are viable in any culture. The obligation rests with the social scientists of all disciplines to sift out the good and necessary constituents of our culture, its real values, and its institutions which are not man-made, from the parts which are not viable in the context of a new society; to set desirable and attainable goals, and to choose the means to reach them. Every available help from within and from without our society must be sought and used. The fear that we may be lost as a cultural or political entity in the world of the future is only too well grounded if our thinking is that we must resist or resent change and merely preserve the past. That is impossible and that way lies stagnation and death.

The tasks of the social psychologist on the basis of present available knowledge can be listed as follows:

1. To search for the survivals of pre-rational mythical or magical thinking in our midst, and by exposing them eradicate them. Mythical or magical thinking means the survival of the non-rational, the fantasy world of society's infancy. Man's history in society should be the history of the gradual emancipation of reason from the infra-rational.

2. To search for and eradicate the hatreds, prejudices, stereotypes, and fears which one generation tries to pass on to the next. All societies tend to perpetuate these irrational

processes, usually under the guise of good and desirable rationalizations. Society must be told that there are no legitimate hatreds or enmities between peoples. The young members of society must be told that there are no legitimate hates or prejudices.

3. To search for and understand the non-rational determinants of behavior which the society uses to bring about conformity of its members to its own demands, whether these be calamitous, such as capital punishment, subtle as with the use of the shame motif to keep up with the neighbors, immoral as when propaganda is substituted for truth or truth itself is subjected to the demands of the state in producing a particular kind of citizen.

4. To study current causes with a view to anticipating their effects on other dimensions of society, to evaluate these by criteria other than those of psychology, to determine whether or not they are desirable and to be encouraged, or undesirable and avoiding action to be taken.

5. To discover by psychological means the self-image a society has of itself, and its validity, and to compare it with the reality, and with the image of a given society as held by another society.

6. To release the individual within the social group from his subjection to the non-rational forces of the group so that he can develop as a person. Many do not even know that they are subjected, and others think their subjection is a good thing.

7. To eliminate all beliefs held on purely emotional grounds.

8. To understand the true nature of man, for whose perfectibility society is what it is.

The strangest thing about the social sciences, and in a

way their glory, is the fact that they alter what they study by the very fact of studying it. The knowledge acquired by the social psychologist rapidly reaches society itself. It is more difficult to cling to an irrational process of prejudice when you know that it is irrational. Gradually, truth prevails.

13 emotional development of the ecclesiastical student

It is probably true to say that emotional life, with its phases of development, its conflicts, and its effects on rational processes, is the most difficult area of personality to cope with, both from the students' and from the director's point of view.

A glance first at the phases of development may help us. The human being, going through the maturation process, passes through a fairly well-defined series of stages, both in the physiological and the psychological orders. Maturation is a linear continuous process from conception to the decline called senility, and passes through infancy, childhood, the latency period, pre-puberty, puberty, adolescence, full maturity, and senescence. To each of these phases there correspond appropriate processes and specific problems, though not a great deal is known about some of them. Mostly, psychologists have studied childhood and adolescence, perhaps because they are particularly attractive, or perhaps because they are more easily studied than adulthood or senescence. It is impossible to set accurate age-limits to these phases, though in general one might date childhood from about two-and-a-half, latency from about five or six, adolescence from the early teens. There is a considerable amount of convincing evidence that adolescence occurs earlier now than it used to. In the case of girls, the menarche occurs on the average four months earlier every decade for the last hundred and twenty years. This means that adolescence in girls is now about four years earlier than it was in mid-nineteenth century. By contrast, the onset of adulthood appears to be getting later, though this would be much harder to prove. It is as if society had agreed to prolong adolescence from the late teens into the middle twenties. If this is so it is enormously important for our understanding of young people. It would mean for example that whereas adolescence a century ago ran from about fifteen to nineteen in the case of girls, it must now be considered as running from about eleven or twelve to twenty-three or four: a twelve-year maturation period instead of a four- or five-year one. Adolescence in boys is more difficult to date, but on the whole there appears to be general agreement that it sets in about two years later than in the case of girls. It does not appear to run two years longer at the upper end, however. In fact it might even be considered to terminate a little earlier, at least in some societies.

But even the figures indicated are subject to great variation. Thus, whereas seventy-two per cent of girls are physiologically mature at thirteen years of age, some twenty per cent will have to wait till they are over fourteen, and six per cent till they reach fifteen before the menarche. In boys the corresponding figures are: 14% mature at 13, 48% at 14 and 78% at 15. These figures are important for our topic, first because they indicate the great difference between boys and girls, and secondly because they indicate the great variation in maturity between boys of the same chronological ages.

In phase with the different stages of maturation, there occur certain rhythmic oscillations of social interest. Thus, at first, the infant naturally makes no distinction between boys and girls. It is socially asexual or simply non-sexual. The child of two or three is bi-sexual, recognizing gradually that there is a difference between boys and girls, but taking no account of this in its social relations with other children. With the approach of the latency period the child withdraws to the shelter of its own sex: not exclusively, not pathologically, but simply as a natural process to allow the next phase of development to occur with the least possible turmoil. This is the stage at which the young boy of six will look on another young boy of six who plays with girls as a "sissy", and the girl of six on her companion who plays with boys as a "tomboy"—or whatever happens to be the familiar term of the peer-group.

Soon, having made some progress through the latency period, the child feels emotionally strong enough to emerge from his own sex-group once more. Thus, boys and girls of seven or eight or nine play happily together, recognizing that they are different but without segregation on this basis (other bases, yes: incompetence at the game, tell-taleism, breach of rule, etc.). This is a bi-sexual or hetero-sexual phase. (The phase of defensive withdrawal into the shelter of one's own sex is called a homosexual phase, but the term must be carefully used in this psychological sense so as to differentiate it sharply from its more usual connotation of sexual perversion. The defensive withdrawal in question here is certainly not a perversion.) From this heterosexual phase, the child passes, with the onset of psychological puberty (a year or two earlier than physiological puberty) or the pre-pubertal phase referred to in our second paragraph, into a new homosexual phase (again, let us repeat that this means a withdrawal into the shelter of one's own sexual peers). It is easy to see that this withdrawal has an impor-

tant biological and psychological function: it enables the
growing organism to take the great leap into sexual maturity
without the disturbing stimuli of the other sex, or at any
rate with these minimized. When the conscious mind of the
growing child has learned, however inadequately, to come
to grips with its new-found sexuality, the adolescent is then
ready to enter the bi-sexual society once again. Thus, towards
the middle of adolescence, one finds once again the child
emerging from the defensive positions of its own sex, and
heterosexual interests and play activities are sought once
again. With this very fore-shortened version of a very complex phenomenon we must be content at this juncture.

The importance of these considerations for our theme
are: (1) they indicate that the youth who comes to us for
ecclesiastical studies, of chronological age seventeen years,
may be at almost any stage of emotional development. Two
per cent of boys reach physiological maturity at seventeen,
two per cent at eleven, and the rest anywhere in between.
Some will thus have had time to come to grips with their
inner conflicts, others will not even have experienced them
yet. (2) Some may have come through to the second heterosexual phase, others may be still in the defensive phase of
withdrawal to the shelter of their own sex, and a few perhaps
may be still in the first heterosexual phase of undisturbed
acceptance of bi-sexual society as in the pre-puberty phase.
By the time these youths will have passed through our hands
some six or seven years later, they will be expected to have
reached a degree of maturity at least as· far advanced as
their co-age group who have not entered the seminary or
religious order. (3) We should not be surprised to find some
—very few perhaps—working their way without difficulty
to full maturity (defined for purposes of this article as the
stage of auto-determination of one's acts plus emotional

control, concepts which will be explained later), while others will have to work their way (but quickly) through the anxieties, conflicts and storms of adolescence. Neither should we be surprised to find that some cannot make it, for they may have a long way to go, and perhaps the very society within which they have to reach maturity may itself be a delaying process.

In the course of his adolescence, the average young person experiences a vague ill-defined complex state of emotion, describable perhaps as a mixture of desires, impulses, curiosity, and anxiety, forming a sort of penumbra on the fringe of consciousness. While this complex state is fundamentally linked with biological maturation, it is not necessarily sexual in the narrow sense. It represents the total affective tone, through which the young person must work his way to three objectives: he must determine his identity, role and status. The achieving of identity means much more than the simple concept of learning who you are: it means discovering one's autonomy as a person, learning both the strengths and weaknesses of one's personality, learning the meaning of human consciousness, with its consequences in self-initiated action, learning to be alone. It means also, in existential terms, learning to respect reality, not in any rhetorical sense, but in the sense of whatever is, is: and for finite creatures, the consequence of this: the total irreversibility of history. Only in this way can auto-determination, intrinsic to maturity, be achieved. And the measure of his respect for reality is the measure of the degree to which one has escaped from the fantasy-needs and satisfactions of adolescence.

Role and status can be considered together. The maturing young person has no innate knowledge of his role in the world, neither in the most general sense of his role as a human being, nor in the more specialized senses of his role as a young man, his sexual role, his role as a student, as a member of society, as an adult, and eventually as a priest. He must learn all these things, and some of them may be difficult. In the seminary he has to come to terms with his adulthood, even before it is reached, while the world around him condones the extension of adolescence into adulthood more and more. He may have difficulty with his masculinity, as many girls have with their femininity, and because of the coming sacrifice of the sexual function, refuse the masculine role. He must be helped to reach adulthood, and taught to fulfill his masculine sexual role (active, strong, goal-seeking, choosing), without the fulfillment of genital sexuality. The best lesson in both spheres is taught by a good model.

In this connection, it is of the utmost importance to distinguish three attitudes to the vocation which the young man thinks he has. He may think of it as a way of life, which will make possible for him a fulfillment, a further stage in development, a completion. Or he may look on it as a problem-solving mechanism: he has an inner problem of his own (does not know what to do with himself, where to turn, how to satisfy the I-want-to-be-a-cowboy daydream, get away from the unsatisfactory domestic or social scene, etc., etc.). Or he may see in the seminary, the order, or the priesthood, a defense. He is scared by the affective penumbra of consciousness referred to above, largely because of the strength of libido which he discerns in it, but chiefly perhaps because of a vaguely neurotic streak of anxiety, running like a vein through the marble of his whole personality.

In the case of the second and third attitudes (problem-solving, defense), there is no doubt that they can co-exist with a genuine "vocation", but they are not signs of it, and they will make it extremely difficult for the individual to reach genuine adulthood. One might go even further and say that it is unlikely that such an individual will in fact reach adulthood at all.

The status of the adolescent and of the young adult is not easily defined in a highly mobile society subject to rapid change. In a relatively closed or static society (such as that of a Buddhist society a generation ago, an under-developed society before Europeanization, or our stereotype of Victorian society at its height), the position of the adolescent vis-à-vis his adult reference group is clearly defined. What he may do, what he may not do, what society expects of him, what his relations with his peer-group and with his elders should be, what he may possess, and what interests are permitted to him, all these and many more dimensions of his status are fairly clearly laid down to him. He must learn them and the sanctions that go with them. But in a highly mobile society in rapid transition, there may be a pretty severe conflict between what the society in which he lives may permit, demand, or oblige him to, and what the immediate representatives of the preceding generation may expect. These latter will on the whole maintain the expectations of their own generation without due acknowledgement of the changes which have occurred with ethical relativism. It is certainly not suggested that there should be any change in essentials, fundamentals, principles, morals. But morals must be distinguished from mores. The mores, or set of habitual rules of good conduct, attitudes, stereotypes, prejudices, and traditions, which are peculiar to a group, are not all necessarily good, and are subject to change in proportion to the pressures to which the group is exposed. In a sense they are constantly undergoing change since all groups are, however slowly, changing. It is important therefore that those in charge of young people should be aware of such change, and should be in a position to distinguish clearly between what is unchanging of its nature (the moral law, the ideal of the priesthood, the meaning of the spiritual life, etc.) and what is of the lesser order of social determination. If we make unessential demands proper to a different order of society on our young people, such demands will appear to them somewhat artificial, or even unintelligible. I refer here to attitudes, allegiances, loyalties, which may have been meaningful, even essential in a way, at one phase of development of a society, but which may very well fail to move people at another phase. Or again, the cultural values of one generation may be supplanted in the next by a more valuable or more sophisticated set, which may seem to the older generation not a gain but a great loss. Perhaps the most striking thing about the young people with whom we are concerned is precisely this cultural change. For we are living in a society which has been subject to greater and more rapid cultural change in a generation or two than in the previous century or more. In a very real sense, the development of the personality can be considered as a response to the demands of the culture in which one lives. (It should be clear that the word culture is used here, not in the sense of "cultured" meaning well-educated etc., but rather in the anthropological sense in which it means the total complex of things, values, traditions, and rules which make up a way of life.) Using the word in this sense, one can say that the culture of the younger generation differs from that of the older generation in the following respects: the younger is international where the older was national, wider in scope where the older was more local, involves the rejection of some traditional values where the older demanded acceptance, is leisured where the older had no leisure, affluent (e.g., vacation abroad) where their parents lived at the subsistence level, middle-class where their parents were peasants. These and other differences place a considerable strain on the older generation, who are tempted to become *laudatores temporis acti,* but this is as nothing to the strain it places on younger people, who, with the best will in the world may find themselves in conflict with a whole culture-pattern because of conflict with perhaps an unessential part of it. Might one suggest that there is an added danger for the ecclesiastic forming young people: the danger of confusing virtue with certain natural phenomena. Thus, it is easy to confuse humility with immaturity, charity with affection, obedience with identification. But especially it is easy to confuse chastity with the natural defenses set up in adolescence by the young person himself in order to cope with his instincts. Thus it is not uncommon to find young people trying by a combination of pseudointellectualism and pseudoasceticism rather than by control, to come to terms with their sexuality. The pseudointellectualism is represented by their attempts to cope, by apparently detached intellectual discussion, with the forces of libido, and the pseudoasceticism is seen in their readiness to undertake still physical punishment (cold, fasting), in preference to the less spectacular but more punitive forms of self-discipline.

Because of the difficulties of coping with instinctual life— especially perhaps because the rational components, intellect and will have not yet achieved even a modicum of control— a young man may have recourse to non-rational defenses. It is here especially that the seminary superior or master of students should be alive to problems. It is only too easy for sublimation to take the place of control, and whereas sublimation is one of the few defenses which can on occasion be healthy, it would clearly be unhealthy for an aspirant to the priesthood and celibacy to depend on it. In general one can list four ways of handling libido: repression, suppression, sublimation, and control. These can exist in a variety of combinations, but they should not be confused with one another. Repression is an unconscious defense whereby the conscious mind defends itself against the anxiety or unpleasantness provoked by libido by keeping it firmly under the threshold of consciousness. It is a denial of reality. Suppression is the ideal of stoic apathy, the detachment of some oriental system, or "la belle indifference" of the hysteric. Control is the function of intellect and will in respect of emotion generally. But sublimation means the directing of the energies associated with libido to acceptable—particularly socially acceptable—ends, so that their force is diminished, and the problems of instinct do not have to be faced in full consciousness (it is essential to remember that sublimation is an unconscious defense, whereas control is essentially a conscious function). During the formative period, while one is preparing for priesthood or profession, the libido can be handled fairly successfully either through fear or anxiety, or by sublimating it through constant and varied activity throughout the day, through preoccupation with symbols, and meticulous attention to rule and ritual. This can the more readily happen when an individual is relieved of the experience of his aloneness, his autonomy as a person, through too great an identification with the group. The more one submerges oneself, one's identity, in the group, the more readily can one abdicate responsibility for one's acts, and thus revert from adulthood to the less mature state of the adolescent. It also happens more readily the more one has come to depend on handling the forces of instinctual life by conceptualizing them intellectually rather than by controlling them voluntarily. Sublimation can easily simulate virtue. But it is essentially a natural subrational defense, not a virtue, and therein lies its danger, for as soon as the goal, ordination or profession, is achieved, this subrational defense may rather suddenly be found to be inadequate. The external mechanism which sustained it and indeed made it possible are removed, and the will is exposed to danger without the strength of acquired habits to sustain it. The liberation (from minutiae of the rule, for instance) which should have freed the will to enable it to perform acts of virtue (self-initiated acts of the mature autonomous person) appears instead to provide ground merely for the operation of a new defense mechanism: rationalization. (When one removes one set of defenses from a patient without curing his condition, i.e. bringing him to maturity, he very often proceeds to erect a new set.) The situation here is somewhat analogous. The natural defenses, rather than natural or supernatural virtues, on which the younger person has depended, are found to be either redundant or inefficacious. He may now rationalize his difficulties by doubting the validity of his ordination, by claiming that he did not really understand what he was doing, or by claiming that the burdens are insupportable anyway. The fear or anxiety (consciously experienced as a fear or anxiety that he might not be called to orders or profession, but unconsciously, a fear of libido itself), which served successfully as counter-affect to the force of libido, has likewise been removed, so that now he has not even the fear of libido to fall back on, and this in turn reinforces the rationalization process.

There is a curious relation between some forms of sexual deviation on the one hand and religiosity or obsessional ritualistic processes on the other. In the case of the homosexual, latent or active, it may be that his basic insecurity (he has as it were by definition not come to terms with his sexuality, his masculinity, his adulthood) finds relief in the security of repetitive performance. Outside religion he would have invented his own private rituals as anxiety-relievers. Within religion, he finds this security provided for him. (I speak here not primarily of the ritual of the Church, the public liturgy, though sometimes that also may be misused for this purpose, but rather of the more exacting meticulous "niggling" sort of ritual which established itself in a closed society over a sufficiently long period of time. Happily this seems to be somewhat rarer than it used to). The primitive psychological function of ritual appears to be the alleviation of the anxieties provoked by the violation of taboo. The inner repudiation of the self finds expression in the de-personalized character of ritualistic performance, and the disturbed emotional life finds expression in emotional piety. It is also possible that some symbols, well known to the psychologist to have an unconscious sexual meaning, and frequently used in an elevated and transformed way in religion, may satisfy very deep-seated and repressed processes in the sexually disturbed: candles, water, vestments, gestures of abasement, punishment, etc. One should be especially wary of any individual who combines effeminacy of personality with apparently esthetic pleasure in ritual.

The majority of our students do not of course present serious emotional problems. Most of them seem to proceed through adolescence to adulthood guided as it were by built-in natural maturation processes. In this chapter we are concerned with the deviations from the norm: a minority in any population, but a particularly distressing one in the group we are dealing with. It may therefore be helpful to try to list some of the prewarning signals that nature has recourse to, in order to prepare us for impending breakdown. It would be a mistake of course to refer all one's problem children to a psychiatrist. But it would be equally wrong to neglect natural means to help those whose problem is strictly on the natural plane. The confessional as such does not "cure" morbid emotional states. It is not necessary that every priest should be an expert in psychopathology, but it is desirable that those in charge of young people should be able to recognize the premonitory signals of coming problems. What follows is a list of some of the more commonly observed indicators of impending emotional trouble. It should be noted that one never sets undue store by a single isolated episode, or a single isolated symptom. What one must look to is the general pattern of an individual's personality and behavior.

General:

(a) Morbid anxiety without a discernible cause, or anxiety out of all proportion to its apparent cause.

(b) Painful or intolerable sadness ("depression") without reasonable cause.

(c) Loss of normal adaptation—e.g., a student who rather suddenly begins to complain that he "cannot concentrate" on anything (this condition must of course be carefully distinguished from straight rationalization of laziness).

(d) Inverse relation between expressed aims or levels of aspiration and actual resources of the personality.

(e) Attempts by sheer physical intensity of endeavor to increase the efficacy of prayer, or to overcome temptation, especially of a reflex organic kind.

(f) Psychosomatic disturbances, e.g., severe headaches without cause, localised anaesthesias, fainting, nausea, or *a fortiori* unidentifiable functional disorders, etc.

(g) Any threat of suicide.

Particular:

The following are examples of significant individual behavioral items complained of by persons in whom emotional disturbances may have developed:

(a) A feeling that someone on the other side of choir is always watching him. (Paranoid process.)

(b) That he is being spoken about behind his back. (Paranoid process.)

(c) That he is subject to some mysterious ray, or any form of *actio in distans*, e.g., telepathy. (Schizoid process.)

(d) That he has a characteristic smell. (Schizoid process.)

(e) That people avoid him because of this. (Schizoid process.)

(f) That he can make other people behave in certain ways (e.g., make them leave the choir, or the chapel, or pick things up, etc.) merely by transferring his thoughts to them. (Schizoid process.)

(g) Any experience of an hallucinatory kind, such as hearing "voices", seeing "visions", etc. (Schizoid process.)

Early Symptoms:

Following is a list of some of the more common symptoms of impending trouble, which it would be an advantage to know about. They correspond on the psychological plane to elementary notions of hygiene such as temperature, rashes, infection, coughing, etc., on the physiological plane.

(a) Prolonged insomnia.

(b) Absurd claims of power, prerogatives, or privileges.

(c) Unhealthy preoccupation with sin, guilt, etc., especially in connection with chastity, to the point of bizarre pulpit behavior (denunciations, irrational obsessive attitude, etc.).

(d) Dissociated processes, such as uncontrollable inappropriate laughter, fugues, amnesia.

(e) Speech disorders (other than stuttering) such as oblique speech, neologisms, bizarre association processes.

(f) Complaints of "peculiar" headaches, e.g., a feeling of being bound by hoops of steel around the head, or feeling of numbness in the skull, etc.

(g) Persecution delusions.

(h) Magical thinking (e.g. I can get rid of this temptation, or pass this examination, etc., if I say such and such a formula three times with the proper amount of concentration, etc., etc.).

Many of our students complain of difficulties in study, and indeed it would appear that sometimes at least their studies seem to give rise to neurotic symptoms. Much of this type of trouble seems to be due to their lack of understanding of some elementary facts about study. It is important that they should understand that there is no learning without hard work. It would appear that many waste valuable time planning how they are going to work tomorrow, making précis they are going to use next year, eliminating material which is "not on the course", etc.

But it is even more important that they should understand that there is no such thing as "brain fag": the human brain does not get tired by studying (though other organs may tire of the process). The eyes do not "get tired reading" (on the average they are at rest at least four-fifths of the time we are reading). A student complaining in this way will always be found ready to go to a film (for a rest?). Students complaining of more absurd symptoms still (e.g., flashing lights, bells ringing in his ears, etc.) are too close to the neurotic and are bad risks for the future. Many of the emotional conflicts which arise about study are perhaps due to the fact that the student clings in a childish way to the possibility of discovering a magic formula which will eliminate the sheer hard work of study. Thus many students confuse obsessional routines (designed to eliminate real study) with order in their work (which is essential for any real study). There is of course an unavoidable anxiety about examinations which must be passed: but it should be made clear to all young people that anxiety is an integral part of human existence. No important function in life can be wholly devoid of anxiety. Directors of students should learn, as psychiatrists have learned and general practitioners are learning, that it is not a good thing to prescribe "a good rest" for students showing the symptoms we have been describing. Any student who needs rest to the point of not being able to live the common life even substantially, is already perhaps ill enough to be sent away.

index